MASADA
Herod's Fortress and the Zealots' Last Stand

Endpapers: Engraving of the southern end of Masada by W.Tipping

MASADA

Herod's Fortress and the Zealots' Last Stand

YIGAEL YADIN

Professor of Archaeology, Hebrew University, Jerusalem
and Director of the Masada Archaeological Expedition

 Steimatzky's Agency Ltd.
Jerusalem

To the volunteer

© 1966 by Yigael Yadin
First Published November 1966
Second Impression February 1967
Third Impression March 1967
Fourth Impression March 1968
Fifth Impression February 1970
Sixth Impression July 1971
Seventh Impression December 1972
Eighth Impression December 1973
Translated from the Hebrew by Moshe Pearlman
Designed by John Wallis for George Weidenfeld and Nicolson Ltd
Phototypeset by BAS Printers Limited, Wallop, Hampshire
Printed by Jarrold and Sons Ltd, Norwich

Contents

Staff members of the expedition

Y. Yadin, M.A., Ph.D. – director of the expedition
D. Bahat, B.A. – field supervisor
Malka Batyevsky, B.A. – in charge of field registry
M. Ben-Dov, B.A. – assistant field supervisor*
A. Ben-Tor, M.A. – field supervisor
Chief Petty Officer M. Cohen – in charge of work safety*
Y. Cohen – assistant field supervisor*
Deborah Dov-Menczel – pottery restorer*
Capt A. Drori, B.A. – field supervisor*
I. Dunayevsky – architect
A. Eitan, B.A. – field supervisor*
Lieut. Col. Y. Eran – administrator (first season)
A. Fagin – assistant field supervisor and in charge of volunteers*
G. Foerster, M.A. – assistant to the director and field supervisor
Lt. Col. D. Gelmond – administrator (second season)
S. Guttman – field supervisor
Rachel Hachlili, M.A. – field supervisor*
A. Kempinski, B.A. – field supervisor*
M. Kochavi, M.A. – field supervisor*
M. Livneh – field supervisor*
M. Magen – assistant field supervisor*
E. Menczel – architect
Z. Meshel, M.A. – field supervisor*
Aviva Rosen – field secretary*
Johanna Salajan-Lamm – draughtswoman
C. Slack – pottery restorer
Y. Shiloh, B.A. – field supervisor*
D. Ussishkin, M.A. – field supervisor*
A. Volk – photographer
J. Voskuil – restorer
Swisan Williams – draughtswoman
Capt Y. Yefet – camp commander
Esther Yuval, B.A. – field supervisor*
Y. Zafrir, B.A. – field supervisor*

* part-time

Preface

The elaborate organization of the Masada expedition was shared by numerous people, organizations and scientific institutions. Proper acknowledgement will be made to all of them in the final scientific publication of the excavations at Masada.

The help of the volunteers and of the Israel Defence Forces is recorded throughout this book. Here I should like to express my sincere thanks to the sponsors of the expedition, who not only made it financially possible, but showed enthusiasm and interest and encouraged us all along: Miriam and Harry Sacher, Terence and the late Mathilda Kennedy, Leonard Wolfson and the Wolfson Foundation, and the *Observer* newspaper and its Editor, David Astor.

It is impossible to mention all the people who were connected with this enterprise in one way or another and to whom I am deeply indebted. However, it is equally impossible to write these lines without mentioning Lajos Lederer and Ronald Harker of the *Observer*; the former for his vital help in the initial stages of planning the expedition and his constant interest; the latter for actually being 'our man in London' throughout the two years of work and for his valuable and wise counsel in all matters connected with the public aspect of the expedition. I am also personally grateful to Mr Harker for reading the manuscript of this book and for the benefit of his advice.

The expedition was carried out on behalf of the Hebrew University, Jerusalem, the Israel Exploration Society and the Department of Antiquities of the Government of Israel. I should like to thank in particular my friend J. Aviram, the honorary secretary of the Israel Exploration Society; had it not been for his initiative and insistence, I doubt if I would have undertaken this enormous task. His unfailing help throughout cannot be overstressed.

The tremendous work of restoration and preservation was done by the Department for Landscaping and the Preservation of Historical Sites and the National Park Authority, under the general direction of Mr Y. Yannai. I wish to put on record my deep appreciation of the work of Mr J. Gasko, who was in charge of the restoration field unit, and Mr M. Yoffe, the chief mason. The reconstruction as a whole was executed in accordance with the recommendations of a special committee whose members were:

I. Dunayevsky, S. Guttman, M. Livneh, E. Menczel, A. Sharon, Y. Yannai and myself.

No archaeological excavation can be carried out successfully without able staff, all the more so under conditions as hard as those at Masada. I was therefore particularly lucky to have with me a group of excellent assistants, whose superb team spirit, sense of humour, devotion and co-operation enabled us to achieve our goal.

The unprecedented interest of the general public in the Masada discoveries – evidenced by the many thousands who have flocked to hear illustrated lectures on the subject in the past two years – is perhaps directly responsible for the writing of this book as well as for its form of text and pictures running together throughout. Most of the black-and-white photographs were taken by the expedition photographer Mr A. Volk and some by the Israeli Air Force, to whom I am indebted. While the majority of coloured photographs were taken by myself, I should like to thank Mr E. Elisofon for the pictures on pages 28, 40, 60–1, 71, 98 and 110 (bottom). Some of the photographs of objects were taken by D. Harris.

My good friend Mr M. Pearlman's intimate knowledge of Masada, enabled him to render more than a literal translation of my Hebrew manuscript by conveying its spirit as well. The excerpts from Josephus come from Whiston's well-known translation; its somewhat archaic style seems to me to be appropriate.

Finally, I should like to thank Carmella, my wife. Single-handed in our 'rear headquarters' in Jerusalem she dealt with all our correspondence and the thousands of volunteer applications. That this book in its present form is better than when I wrote it is mainly due to her.

YIGAEL YADIN
Jerusalem, 1966

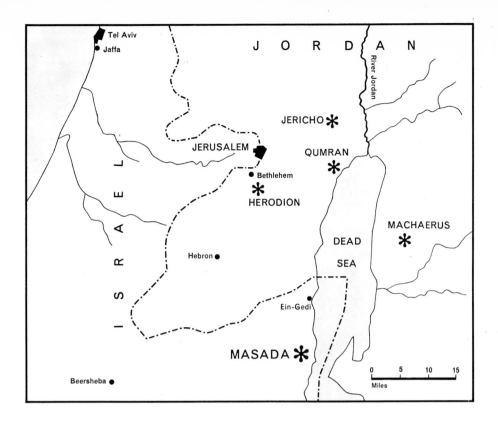

Map of the Dead Sea area showing Masada.

1 The challenge

The rock of Masada, at the eastern edge of the Judean desert with a sheer drop of more than 1,300 feet to the western shore of the Dead Sea, is a place of gaunt and majestic beauty. It is also the site of one of the most dramatic episodes in Jewish history.

In the 1st century AD Palestine was under the occupation of the Romans, who had overthrown the Jewish Maccabean kingdom in the middle of the previous century. Periodic rebellion by the inhabitants, who sought to regain their freedom and sovereignty, had been quickly crushed. But in the year 66 AD the Jewish revolt flared up into a full-scale country-wide war, which raged with fierce bitterness for four years, the Romans having to bring in legion after legion of reinforcements to suppress the insurgents. In 70 AD the Roman general Titus conquered Jerusalem, sacked the city, destroyed the Temple, and expelled the bulk of the Jewish survivors from the country.

One outpost alone held out till 73 AD – the fortress of Masada. According to the 1st-century historian Josephus Flavius, the first to fortify this natural defensive position was 'Jonathan the High Priest', and there was controversy among scholars as to which Jonathan he had in mind. But there was no controversy at all about the man who turned Masada into the formidable fort it became: King Herod the Great. Between the years 36 and 30 BC, Herod built a casemate wall round the top, defence towers, storehouses, large cisterns filled ingeniously by occasional rain water, barracks, arsenals and palaces. It was these fortifications and buildings which served the last band of Jewish fighters in their struggle against the Romans some seventy-five years after Herod's death.

At the beginning of the 66 AD rebellion, a group of Jewish zealots had destroyed the Roman garrison at Masada and held it throughout the war. They were now – after the fall of Jerusalem – joined by a few surviving patriots from the Jewish capital who had evaded capture and made the long arduous trek across the Judean wilderness, determined to continue their battle for freedom. With Masada as their base for raiding operations, they harried the Romans for two years. In 72 AD, Flavius Silva, the Roman Governor, resolved to crush this outpost of resistance. He marched on Masada with his Tenth Legion, its auxiliary troops and thousands of prisoners of war carrying water, timber and provisions across the stretch of

Opposite: The rock of Masada from the north.

barren plateau. The Jews at the top of the rock, commanded by Eleazar ben Yair, prepared themselves for defence, making use of the natural and man-made fortifications, and rationing their supplies in the storehouses and cisterns.

Silva's men prepared for a long siege. They established camps at the base of the rock, built a circumvallation round the fortress, and on a rocky site near the western approach to Masada they constructed a ramp of beaten earth and large stones. On this they threw up a siege tower and under covering fire from its top they moved a battering ram up the ramp and directed it against the fortress wall. They finally succeeded in making a breach.

This was the beginning of the end. That night, at the top of Masada, Eleazar ben Yair reviewed the fateful position. The defensive wall was now consumed by fire. The Romans would overrun them on the morrow. There was no hope of relief, and none of escape. Only two alternatives were open: surrender or death. He resolved 'that a death of glory was preferable to a life of infamy, and that the most magnanimous resolution would be to disdain the idea of surviving the loss of their liberty'. Rather than become slaves to their conquerors, the defenders – 960 men, women and children – thereupon ended their lives at their own hands. When the Romans reached the height next morning, they were met with silence. And thus says Josephus at the end of his description:

And so met (the Romans) with the multitude of the slain, but could take no pleasure in the fact, though it were done to their enemies. Nor could they do other than wonder at the courage of their resolution, and at the immovable contempt of death which so great a number of them had shown, when they went through with such an action as that was.

This was the site at which I was privileged to head an eleven months' archaeological expedition in two seasons of exhaustive excavations: from

A volunteer from Britain . . . complete with umbrella.

Poised above a thousand foot precipice, an Israeli volunteer is rope-tied for safety.

The excavation areas were connected by field telephone, here operated by an Israeli girl.

October 1963 to May 1964 and again from November 1964 to April 1965. *Significance of excavations*
I say 'privileged' because it had been the dream of every Israeli archaeologist to fathom the secrets of Masada; and because an archaeological dig here was unlike an excavation at any other site of antiquity. Its scientific importance was known to be great. But more than that, Masada represents for all of us in Israel and for many elsewhere, archaeologists and laymen, a symbol of courage, a monument to our great national figures, heroes who chose death over a life of physical and moral serfdom.

It was therefore with considerable eagerness that I accepted the invitation of the Hebrew University of Jerusalem, the Israel Exploration Society and the Israel Government Department of Antiquities to lead the Masada Archaeological Expedition.

Because of the special appeal of Masada, and also because of the unusual *How the volunteers* difficulties occasioned by its relative inaccessibility, its remoteness in the *were chosen* wilderness, and its harsh climate, we resolved at the very outset of our planning stage to go beyond the customary method of gathering a crew adopted by normal archaeological expeditions. In addition to securing a nucleus of hired labourers, we hit on the idea of inviting volunteers to join us from among the Masada enthusiasts in Israel and overseas. And, indeed, one of the greatest surprises – and delights – of the enterprise, long before we had put scoop to rubble, was the response. A brief announcement in the local press and in the *Observer* of London, together with a series of brilliant articles written by Patrick O'Donovan, brought thousands of replies from volunteers, Jews and non-Jews in twenty-eight countries, anxious to take part in the dig. This was all the more remarkable, and a reflection of the enchantment and attraction of Masada, in that our announcement had soberly and specifically stated our conditions of acceptance: volunteers would have to pay their own fares to and from Israel; they would have to stay for at least two weeks; the living would be rough – tented accommodation with ten beds to a tent, and the food far from cordon-bleu

An Irish volunteer at work on the lower terrace of Herod's villa.	Another British volunteer, sifting earth near the hoard of shekels.	This Danish nurse cleared the 'swimming pool' single-handed.	The broom held by this Danish member of the expedition was used for cleaning finds.

The expedition tents at the foot of the Roman ramp. Silva's camp is outside the picture, immediately to the left.

standard. (I should add right away that we lived up to our conditions!) And still we were flooded with applications.

In addition to individuals from Israel and abroad, we also received groups of Israeli volunteers from the Defence Forces, who were changed every two weeks; from *Gadna* – a form of Junior O.T.C. composed of senior secondary school pupils; and from the youth of our *kibbutzim* (communal farm villages), who could come for only a week at a time.

This volunteer system enabled us to run twenty-three fortnightly 'shifts' throughout the two seasons of excavations. Together with the teams of professional archaeologists, administration, and restoration crew – the restoration project was another unique feature about which I shall have something to say later – we averaged 300 participants all the time. In a world where the spirit of idealism is generally thought to be declining, the Masada expedition showed that it was still very much alive.

Pottery assembly point; at the end of a day's work, pottery was brought down by cable ferry, washed, marked and assembled.

2 The task

All that had been known of Masada's dramatic past had come to us from one source alone: the writings of that brilliant historian and unfortunate Jew, Josephus Flavius (Yoseph ben Matatyahu, in Hebrew). At the beginning of the great revolt in 66 AD, Josephus had been one of the Jewish commanders in Galilee. Later he went over to the Romans. Yet no one could have matched his gripping description of what took place on the summit of Masada on that fateful night in the spring of 73 AD. Whatever the reasons, whether pangs of conscience or some other cause which we cannot know, the fact is that his account is so detailed and reads so faithfully, and his report of the words uttered by Eleazar ben Yair is so compelling, that it seems evident that he had been genuinely overwhelmed by the record of heroism on the part of the people he had forsaken. (Two women on Masada had failed to go through with Eleazar's plans and had remained hidden, emerging when the Roman soldiers appeared. They told them what had happened, and Josephus no doubt heard it from the Romans, though it is not ruled out that he also interviewed the survivors.) It would be one of the tasks of our archaeological expedition to see what evidence we could find to support the Josephus record.

Josephus, the only source of history of Masada

Before beginning with a description of the excavations and the discoveries, I must clarify two points which are essential to an understanding of the nature of the Masada we came to study. The first concerns its main builder, Herod. Josephus, as I have said, indicates that the first to fortify it was Jonathan the High Priest, though scholars have been divided as to whether he was referring to the brother of Judah the Maccabee (middle of 2nd century BC) or another Jonathan: Alexander Jannaeus (who reigned 103–76 BC), who was known in Hebrew as Jonathan. But all are agreed that the main structures and fortifications are the work of King Herod; this is what Josephus has to say:

Masada built by Herod as a royal citadel

> For the report goes how Herod thus prepared this fortress on his own account, as a refuge against two kinds of danger; the one for fear of the multitude of the Jews, lest they should depose him and restore their former kings to the government; the other danger was greater and more terrible, which arose from Cleopatra, Queen of Egypt, who did not conceal her intentions, but spoke often to Antony, and desired him to cut off Herod, and entreated him to bestow the Kingdom of Judea upon her. And certainly it is a great wonder that Antony did never comply

with her commands in this point, as he was so miserably enslaved to his passion for her; nor should anyone have been surprised if she had been gratified in such her request. So the fear of these dangers made Herod rebuild Masada.

This is a most important point. Scholars did not always support this thesis of Josephus, and some sought to explain the work at Masada as an attempt by Herod to incorporate it into the general defence line of his kingdom. Here, I think, the result of our excavations shows clearly that Josephus was right. At all events, he was certainly right in arguing that Masada was turned into a personal royal citadel and not an ordinary fortification. This alone can explain the fact that in addition to the walls and storehouses necessary to all citadels, the principal features of Masada's complex of buildings are two palaces, one more magnificent than the other. The sight of them is particularly spectacular, set as they are atop a bare rock in the heart of the wilderness. It is evident, therefore, that Herod prepared Masada as a refuge for himself and his family, erecting buildings on a scale of grandeur suited to the standard of living to which he had become accustomed elsewhere. For Herod, at least, Masada was a royal citadel, and it is as such that we must view it today if we are to fathom the secret of its structures.

Period of Zealots' defence of Masada

The second point that needs special mention concerns the period of the Zealots' defence of Masada. We knew from the writings of Josephus that after the death of Herod, Masada was garrisoned by Roman legionaries, and that these were wiped out in the year 66 AD by Menahem, a leader of the revolt, who captured Masada. We also knew that with its fall to the Romans in 73 AD, Flavius Silva left a garrison there. Surveys previous to ours had shown further that in the 5th and 6th centuries AD a small settlement of monks was located on the site and that they had built a modest chapel and lived in miserable dwellings and caves. What, we wondered, before starting the dig, would we find of the period of the Zealots? What could be left apart from the cinders of the great fire described by Josephus?

In the event, the discovery of the remains of the Masada defenders proved to be one of the most impressive experiences of the expedition. They had left behind no grand palaces, no mosaics, no wall paintings, not even anything that could be called buildings, for they had simply added primitive partitions to the Herodian structures to fit them as dwellings, and there they had installed their domestic items, like clay ovens and wall couches, which we came across. But to us, as Jews, these remains were more precious than all the sumptuousness of the Herodian period; and we had our greatest moments when we entered a Zealotian room and under a layer of ashes came upon the charred sandals of small children and some broken cosmetic vessels. We could sense the very atmosphere of their last tragic hour. This feeling was heightened when we excavated a palace room decorated with Herodian Roman wall paintings – which had been covered by soot from an oven which had been put up in a corner. This, more than any of the other remains, revealed the vast contrast between the Masada of the year 66 AD and the Masada of Herod. The Zealots and their families had

Masada from the west: the Dead Sea and the
mountains of Moab are in the background.

no need of luxurious palaces. They faced the brutal challenge of life or
death, the stark problem of existence, and Herodian magnificence meant
nothing to them.

What follows in these pages are our discoveries – both the remains of the
material glory of Herod and the moving relics of the Zealots, who made of
Masada a symbol. The illustrations accompanying the text are photographs taken during the excavations, most of them at the very moment of
discovery. It is not my purpose to offer a dry scientific record; rather is it to
enable the reader to share our remarkable experience.

3 Getting to work

Problems of choosing a site for the camp

For months before the start of the expedition we pondered the problem of where to set up our base camp of some forty to fifty tents. At the eastern foot of Masada? On the summit? On the west? We visited the site time and again with Israeli Army engineers – the army had taken upon itself to carry out part of the work of establishing the base camp – and we finally decided on the western location. We did not feel it proper to base ourselves on the top of the rock – the area of the main excavations – for, apart from other problems, using it as a dwelling area for hundreds of workers was likely to spoil the site. On the face of it, the most convenient spot was at the eastern foot of the rock, close to the youth hostel, where there is a good water supply and electricity. It is also served by the asphalt road which runs from S'dom northwards to Ein Gedi. Moreover, at this site we would also enjoy the help of Yehuda Almog, chairman at the time of the local regional council, who had devoted all his adult life to the Dead Sea area and who was one of those who had been trying to persuade me for years to undertake the Masada dig.

But these were only surface advantages. The drawbacks were serious. The site here was 1,200 feet below the summit, and we would have to climb up and down the tortuous 'snake path' which winds its way round the eastern escarpment of Masada, the very path whose 'stumbling-blocks' are so dramatically described by Josephus. This would probably not have bothered some of the younger members of the expedition, but for me and others it would have been something of an effort to make the steep fifty-minute climb at least once and possibly more each day. But what really decided us against this eastern location was the extreme difficulty, from here, of hauling to the top the heavy equipment required for the excavations. We were thus driven to pick the western site. Here, over the Roman ramp which Flavius Silva's soldiers laid with the help of thousands of Jewish prisoners of war, runs a footpath by which the summit of Masada may be reached in only ten minutes. Why, then, do I say 'driven' to choose this spot as our base camp? The fact is that this easy accessibility – a decisive virtue – was its only advantage. Everything else was against it, most particularly the absence of anything that could be called a road. The one route to it was from the west, through the 'Zealots' Ascent', and even that was not more than a rough track, full of boulders and deep ruts, with

Opposite: Airview of Masada from south to north. The snake path is on the eastern cliff and the Roman ramp on the western. In the distance are the oasis of Ein-Gedi and the Dead Sea.

steep wadis to negotiate. Nor was this site served by water or electricity.

However, once we had decided that this was where our camp would be, we bent all our efforts to furnish it with the basic amenities. The army engineers blasted a track through from the south, but this could be only a temporary route, and in fact it did not stand up to the unprecedentedly heavy rains; we had therefore to abandon it and reach Masada via the 'Zealots' Ascent' on vehicles with four-wheel drive – which suffered badly from the experience. Electricity was comparatively simple; we installed generators on the site. Our biggest problem was water, and it took a long time to solve. We installed water-tanks at the base with the idea of filling them each day with tankers or other heavy trucks bringing water from a point many miles away; but the state of the tracks made such regular journeys impossible. Then, to our delight, we discovered about four miles to the west a pipeline belonging to the Naphta Oil Company. There had been some drilling in the area some years earlier, and the pipe had been abandoned. The Mekorot National Water Company came to our help and laid and

Masada from the west with Silva's camp in the foreground:
the ramp is on the right and the Dead Sea on the left.

fitted a thinner pipe to the Naphta pipeline, and so we were able to receive a constant supply by gravity flow. (Our camp was hundreds of feet lower than the plateau to the west; but as a matter of fact the piped-in water even reached the Masada summit.)

The specific siting of the camp also posed a problem. This, again, would not seem to have been difficult, for we had the whole area to choose from. But the ideal spot had already been chosen by Flavius Silva, commander of the Roman Tenth Legion, 1,900 years earlier! He was the first, and he took full advantage of it. His camp, which is extraordinarily well-preserved, has itself become an archaeological site, and if we had established ourselves there, we would have destroyed it. We had to go elsewhere. But the entire area south of Silva's camp was broken by dry river-beds, unsuitable for a base compound the size of ours. However, what Silva lacked, we had: bulldozers, and the will and skill of the army's Engineer Corps. With their help the ground was levelled and prepared for our base camp. Three huts as offices for the expedition and several tents for the permanent staff were put up at the southern extremity, and at the northern end, hard by the Roman camp, we set up the tents for the volunteers. Between the two sections of our compound was the dining hall. In the first season this was a large tent; in the second it was a less primitive structure.

The sight of the adjoining camps, Silva's and our own, was not without its symbolism, and it expressed far more pungently than scores of statements something of the miracle of Israel's renewed sovereignty. Here,

Site chosen beside former Roman camp

Volunteers climbing the ramp at dawn. On the right is the cable ferry, and on top of the ramp the water pipeline which supplied water by gravitation to the summit.

21

Aerial view of Masada, from the west: Silva's camp F is at
the bottom left, and the expedition barracks on the right.
Overleaf: Silva's camp viewed from Masada.

23

cheek by jowl with the ruins of the camp belonging to the destroyers of Masada, a new camp had been established by the revivers of Masada.

Our working day started at dawn and we climbed to Masada by the path across the ramp, beneath a cable-way for heavy equipment which had been erected by the army engineers. The view of Masada from the west is very different from the more familiar one from the east. On the left, there is the northern point of the rock with its three terraces; on the right, the deep Wadi Masada. Reaching Masada by this route each day we could see to our left, on the western slope, remains of the powerful project of Herod – the water system. What we saw were two rows of what looked like dark holes, one series above the other. These were openings to huge cisterns which had been scooped out of the rock, each with a capacity of up to 140,000 cubic feet and altogether totalling close to 1,400,000. How did Herod and his engineers think of filling these cisterns, when there was not then – nor is there today – any spring near Masada, and the rainfall is so rare and meagre? Their solution reflected sheer genius, and like so many ingenious solutions, the concept was simple but the execution very difficult. They based their plan on the existence of two small wadis which pass to the north and the south of Masada. They constructed dams in two places, and from these dams they laid open channels to the two sets of excavated cisterns, one from the southern wadi to the top row, and the second aqueduct from the northern wadi to the bottom row. It was their assumption that with the rains, the water would be held up by the dams and by gravity flow would stream along the aqueducts and fill up the cisterns one after the other.

Another set of cisterns was excavated at the top of Masada and these

Herod's water system

A Byzantine gate on the top of Masada: the helicopter in the background brought supplies when Masada was cut off by floods from the rest of the country.

Opposite: Dramatic view of the northern cliff of Masada from the west. Two rows of cisterns are clearly visible in the centre and above them the track leading to Herod's three-terraced villa.

Before the storm; the ramp still gleaming in the sun.

were filled with the water from the lower cisterns which was brought up by the 'electric' power of those days – thousands of slaves and beasts of burden who carried up the water in jars along two paths, from west and east, which ended by joining the 'snake path'. A simple plan. A plan of genius! Yet when one stands near Masada today in the broiling sun, the area all around bare and burnt, the wadis dry, and no source of water welling forth anywhere in the vicinity, the plan seems illusory, one that could never have worked.

Both during our first and second seasons, we were afflicted by particularly harsh winters. These were a blessed boon to the country, after several years of drought, but for us at Masada they were grim. Many times the southern wind reached gale force of over sixty miles an hour and tore our tents to shreds. Torrential rains which burst from the skies without warning filled the ravines in a flash, and even the wadi between our dining hall and the volunteers' tents became a river, isolating the two sections of our camp. All the wadis west of Masada, including those crossing the Beersheba–Arad road, also overflowed their banks, and the new highway to Arad crumbled in several places, cutting us off from the rest of the country. There were days when the only way in which we could receive our basic supplies was by helicopter. There were days when we had to stop digging

Opposite : One of the huge cisterns excavated from solid rock which supplied water to Masada. A sunbeam streams through the hole below the ceiling from which the water filled the cistern. The staircase is on the right.

29

because the ground had turned to mud. All this was very trying. It must be remembered, too, that the tents were full of water and the clothes the volunteers had brought with them utterly soaked, with no prospect of drying them quickly. Yet despite everything, morale was high. And there were two consolations: first, we witnessed a rare natural spectacle when the two wadis which had supplied the water to the Herodian channels serving the cisterns suddenly filled up and burst their banks.

The aqueducts themselves have long been destroyed; the southern one lies buried beneath the great earth ramp constructed by the Romans, and the northern channel was ruined in several places in the course of time. And so the water of the wadis streamed to waste, and instead of being harnessed by drainage ditches, leapt towards the Dead Sea in a series of breath-taking waterfalls.

In the driving rain, we of the permanent staff and the volunteers would rush to see these falls and gaze in rapt wonder at such marvels of nature. Equally exciting was the visual evidence of how Herod's water supply system worked. If the aqueducts had still been in good repair, all the cisterns excavated in the slope of the Masada rock would have filled up in only a few hours.

We were also able to confirm another item in the writings of Josephus which had seemed to many scholars to be legendary: Josephus says that before the reign of Herod, years before he fortified Masada, Herod's brother Joseph plus members of his family found refuge at Masada. Holding out against the troops of the last of the Hasmoneans and his allies, *Effects of rain confirmed an account by Josephus*

Opposite: The dry river gushing with sudden torrents. It was this *wadi* which supplied water to the rock-hewn cisterns.

Left: Rare scene in the desert: a powerful waterfall at the end of the now broken canal which originally filled up the cisterns.

31

the Parthians, they were about to die of thirst, when suddenly the heavens opened and all the pits that had been in Masada filled with water, and Joseph and his people were saved.

This report in Josephus had been hard to believe; for even if one could imagine the waters of the wadis piling up to fill the cisterns from the rains of Masada – or more particularly from the westward flowing rain-water of the Judean hills – it was difficult to conceive that direct rain over the Masada summit would be enough to fill its clefts. Yet I recall one of those days when we all had to rush for shelter from a sudden downpour. When it was over, I was astonished to behold that the lower-lying areas of the summit were now one huge pool of water. If I had not myself photographed this sight, I would not have believed that it had been taken at the top of Masada. So this story of Josephus had evidently also been based on reliable information.

While I am on the subject of unusual natural phenomena, I shall mention one more which occurred literally during the very last tragic moments before the fall of Masada as described at length by Josephus. He tells how in the final stage of the siege, when the Zealots built a wooden wall to stop up the breach the Romans had effected above the ramp, the Romans threw firebrands and set the wood alight. Suddenly, the direction

An unusual view of the summit. The puddles after the rain confirm Josephus' description.

Flowers on the summit of Masada – an almost immediate result of the rains.

Another of Josephus'
stories confirmed

of the wind changed and began blowing from the north, thus driving the flames on to the Romans. Then, as if at divine injunction, the wind changed direction again and the flames were driven inwards. The Romans saw this as the work of their gods who had come to their help.

Again, a story which would seem difficult to understand, or accept. Yet again, we, the first dwellers at Masada after 1,900 years, living there altogether eleven months, became well aware, from harsh experience, of the vagaries of its weather. The normal strong wind at Masada is southerly or south-westerly, and it was apparently blowing in this direction when the Romans flung their lighted torches at the wooden wall. But we ourselves saw on several occasions how this wind would suddenly veer right round and blow from the north, because of the configuration of the nearby mountains, and as suddenly switch again to blow strongly from the south. Those of us who recalled the Josephus description found in it some compensation for the irksomeness of the changing gusts and the dust that swirled in their wake.

I said earlier that there were two consolations for the tough winters we encountered on our dig. The second was a new and rare beauty for Masada and the Judean desert. As a result of the unusually heavy rains, they were turned in a short time into expanses of green, shot through with flowers.

I also took another photograph at the top of Masada. It could easily be taken for a snapshot of one of the country's national parks. How pleasant it was to roam the ruins of Masada adorned by flowers of every colour. The fruitfulness of Masada's soil, as reflected by such rapid plant-growth, also served to confirm Josephus' words:

The king [Herod] reserved the top of the hill, which was of a fat soil and better mould than any valley, for agriculture, that such as committed themselves to this fortress for their preservation, might not even there be destitute of food, in case they should ever be in want of it from abroad.

It is likely that they raised only vegetables and not trees, but it is probable that trees too could grow there. One of our precious moments was planting pomegranate bushes in a high wind atop Masada during a festive ceremony on the Jewish New Year for Trees (15th of the Hebrew month Shevat). They 'took' well, and when we left the site at the end of the excavations they were flourishing.

However, much of the discomforts from the weather occurred not during the few weeks of gale and storm but during the many months under the burning sun and the rapid transition from heat to cold. Most of the volunteers from European countries suffered less from the rains than from the heat, and the most persuasive evidence of this is the picture showing them in their 'normal' garb in the blazing sun. There was a feeling at times that the volunteers – the women at least – were concerned as much with exposing the present as with uncovering the past.

The main difficulty of living at Masada after a short period
of rain is the heat. A bikini is one solution.

4 The site

The narrow path along the Roman ramp which we would take each morning did not reach the summit of Masada – for the ramp itself, as Josephus had reported, did not terminate at the top of the rock. The connecting link, an earlier track, was no longer serviceable, having been damaged in a series of earth tremors; so the army engineers erected a stairway (wooden steps and metal frame) running from the end of the ramp path right up to the top. With justice did Southern Command and the Engineer Corps affix their emblems. They were proud of their work, and they had the right to be proud, not only for putting up this stairway on the sheer face of the cliff, but also for installing a similar stairway to the cliff-hanging northern palace, in conditions of considerable danger in the broiling summer months of 1963.

When we climbed the steps above the ramp and reached the western edge of Masada, at first we saw no structure with any recognisable plan. The entire area was covered with mounds of stone and rubble and 'we could not see the buildings for the stones'. In order to have an impression of the shape of Masada and its ruins, it is best to look at the photograph taken before the excavations: this photograph was taken from south to north. At the right is the winding 'snake path' on the eastern slope; at the left is the earth ramp on the western slope; at the top is the northern edge of the summit, and at the bottom the southern extremity. As can be seen, the site is a rough rhomboid, shaped rather like a ship, with a very narrow prow in the north, somewhat less narrow in the south, and broad in the centre. It measures some 1,900 feet from north to south and 650 feet from east to west. The picture already indicates that apart from its northern tip, the rest of Masada is surrounded by a casemate wall, that is, a double wall divided by partition walls into a series of rooms or casemates. Most of Masada's buildings are concentrated in the northern half of the summit. The southern half, lower than the rest, was bare for the most part, at least in Herod's time, and was possibly used to raise vegetables.

A clearer impression of the site can be gained by glancing at the photograph, taken from north to south, on page 10: the 'snake path' is on the left and the ramp on the right. The northern edge with its three-tiered palace is in the immediate foreground, and just above it we see the main cluster of Masada's buildings, comprising the formidable storehouses and

The Roman ramp stops short of the summit of Masada. The remaining part was bridged with a staircase by Israeli Army Engineers.

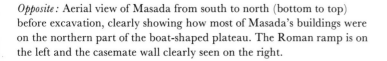

Opposite: Aerial view of Masada from south to north (bottom to top) before excavation, clearly showing how most of Masada's buildings were on the northern part of the boat-shaped plateau. The Roman ramp is on the left and the casemate wall clearly seen on the right.

other structures. On the right, at the centre of the western edge of the rock, is a conspicuous building – actually the largest building on Masada – about which we shall also have much to say.

The coloured plan below roughly corresponds to the aerial photo and emphasises the main structures. We need not at this stage spend much time on the details, but each colour represents a different type of building – storehouse, palace, dwelling room and so on. Even though at first glance the buildings do not seem to have been erected according to any plan and without any considerations of topography, the facts are otherwise. The

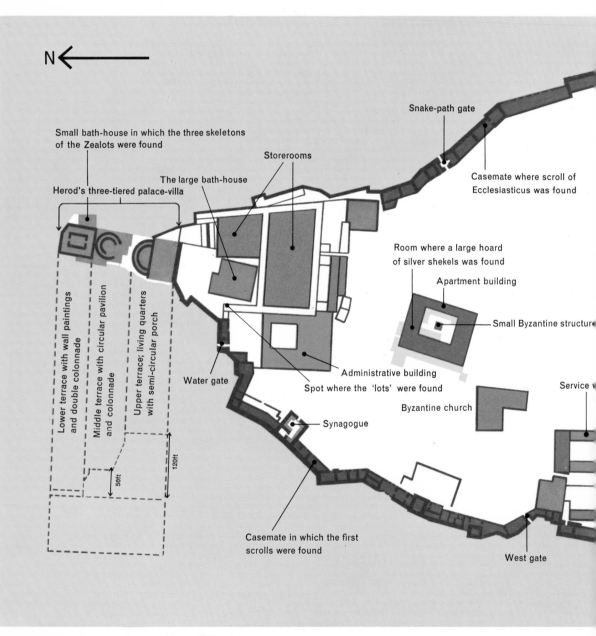

General plan of Masada.

important buildings, as we have seen, are grouped in the north, on the highest ground of Masada, which was comparatively easier to defend. The remaining structures, the palaces scattered here and there, were built on locations higher than their surroundings. The unevenness of the ground does not show on the aerial photographs, but in fact there are hollows and mounds.

In our description of the buildings, in the light of our archaeological discoveries, we shall proceed from north to south, ending with our excavation of the casemate wall running some 4,250 feet round the top of Masada.

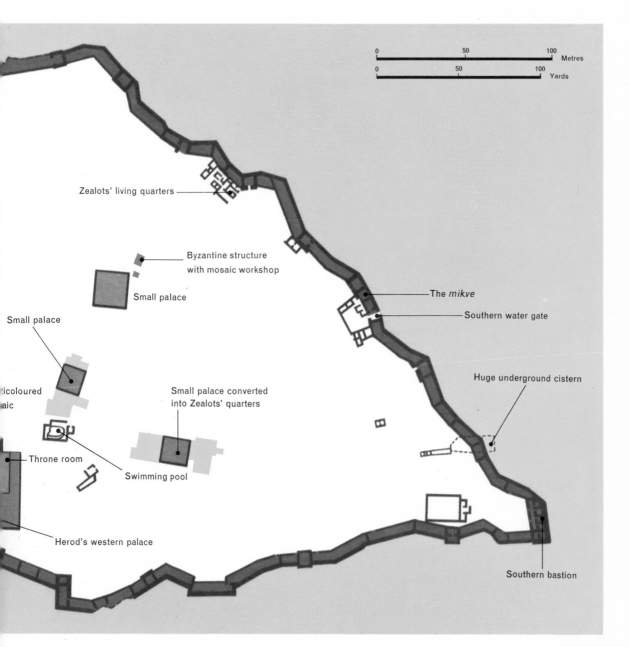

5 The northern palace-villa

One of the Herodian buildings described at length by Josephus, which has aroused the curiosity of scholars who have visited Masada over the last hundred years, was the royal palace. Josephus says this about it:

Josephus' description of the Herodian palace

Moreover, he built a palace therein at the western ascent: it was beneath the walls of the citadel but inclined to its north side. Now, the wall of this palace was very high and strong, and had at its four corners towers sixty cubits high. The furniture also of the edifices, and of the cloisters, and of the baths, was of great variety, and very costly; and these buildings were supported by pillars of single stones on every side: the walls also and the floors of the edifices were paved with stones of several colours. He also had cut many and great pits, as reservoirs for water out of the rocks, at every one of the places that were inhabited, both above and around about the palace and before the wall; and by this contrivance he endeavoured to have water for several uses, as if there had been fountains there. Here was also a road digged from the palace, and leading to the very top of the mountain which yet could not be seen by such as were without [the walls].

Where was this wonderful palace? Up until the 1950s, it was thought to be the large building at the western edge which we mentioned earlier. Chief proponent of this view, who investigated and wrote a considerable amount about it, was the German scholar Schulten. At the beginning of the fifties, not long after the establishment of the State of Israel, Schulten's theory was seriously challenged. The proper identification of this building must be credited to the Israeli youth movements who started trekking to Masada and sought to fathom its secrets. Micha Livne and Shmaryahu Guttman were the first, as far as we know, to climb to the top of Masada not from the west, nor from the east, but from the north. The ascent was indeed difficult, but it enabled them to examine at close quarters the ruins of the strange buildings which had long been visible from a distance by all who had gazed up at the three terraces in the rock, thought to be part of the fortifications. When they reached the top, they immediately concluded, correctly, that these buildings, constructed at the narrowest part of Masada on the very edge of the escarpment, were none other than the ruins of the royal palace described by Josephus.

Theories of the locality of Herod's palace

The search for the true location of this palace was not accidental, despite the majority view of scholars that it was the large building in the west. For that structure, though the largest on Masada, did not fit the

Opposite: An aerial view from the north of the three terraces of Herod's hanging villa after excavation. The supporting wall (see close up in the photograph on page 43) is visible below the lower terrace.

details in Josephus' description. True it was sited in the west, but it was not beneath the wall; it was inside it. Nor did it face north. Most important, there were no signs of the pathway cut in the rock to serve its various levels. These difficulties were of course apparent also to the earlier scholars, but they sought to explain them away by suggesting that on these points, as on other details, the account of Josephus was not accurate.

Josephus' account confirmed

The revelations of the 1950s and the excavations which followed proved that on these points, too, the description of Josephus is very faithful. A glance at the photograph shows immediately that the buildings were constructed in three tiers. The upper terrace is but an extension of the narrow section of the summit, and it is indeed the highest point on Masada. The middle terrace is about sixty feet lower down, and it bears the remains of a circular structure. The bottom terrace – the most northerly – is some forty-five feet below the middle tier, and here, too, one can see ruins, the ruins of a square building with pillars.

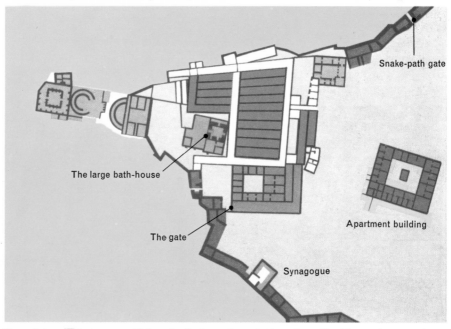

Plan of the northern part of Masada. It shows how the hanging villa (shown in mauve) sticks out like a boat's prow. The large bath-house is shown in pale blue; the storerooms in red; and the administrative building in orange.

The lower terrace

We begin our description of this magnificent structure with the lowest terrace. The rock of Masada tapers to the north and is at its narrowest at this spot – not more than a few yards wide. In order to erect anything at all upon it, Herod's engineers had to fashion some kind of artificial platform with the aid of powerful supporting walls, up to eighty feet in height, hanging over the abyss.

In the 1955–6 survey (see chapter nineteen) important parts of the palace had been excavated and examined, and it was already clear then that the lower parts of the walls on this terrace were decorated with wall paintings. These had been preserved, mostly in the south-west corner. However, owing to lack of time and means, these earlier archaeological survey teams had not managed to uncover the entire site and so, as can be imagined, this was one of our first tasks at the outset of our excavation. We wondered whether the paintings had been preserved on all the walls of this bottom terrace, and if so in what state they were.

To find out, we had to get there; and in order to get there and bring with us the tools and equipment needed for a thorough excavation of the site, army engineers constructed for us a set of wooden steps up the sheer north-western slope of Masada. Sections of the rock had to be blasted into appropriate shapes to support some of the steps, and it was altogether an ingenious and hazardous operation on the part of the engineers.

Huge supporting wall of the lower terrace of the
hanging villa built on the precipice.

43

The magnificent frescoes discovered on the southern part of the lower
terrace. In the foreground are the panels at the base of the inner columns;
in the background the panels and columns seen in the picture opposite.
Opposite: Photograph taken just before discovery of the wall paintings on the
lower terrace. The plastered columns of the southern façade are visible.

After we had cleared the piles of debris, we reached the level from which (and below which) we would be proceeding to uncover the wall paintings – if there was still anything to uncover. Excitement rose among the excavators. A photograph, taken a few days later, shows the section of the terrace with its excavation completed. And it is indeed possible to see the wall paintings. They have kept well during the last 2,000 years. They may not accord with our artistic tastes today, but they represent the style that was widely popular throughout the Roman empire in that era. Similar paintings, though not so well preserved, have been discovered in several other structures in the country belonging to the Herodian period, notably in Samaria, Jericho, Caesarea, and also in Herodion, the fortified tomb of Herod in the Judean desert, not far from Masada. The principal purpose of the artists was to give the lower part of the plastered walls the appearance of being panelled in stone and marble. Their almost desperate attempt to

Discovery of the wall paintings

45

Close-up of the corner of the inner row of columns. The artists' efforts
to imitate the veins of marble are characteristic of the period.

achieve this aim is particularly evident in the walls backing the inner
pillars on this bottom terrace, as may be seen in the picture above.

Lines are painted to look like the veins in marble. This is how the artists
decorated the whole of the lower part of the outer, as well as the inner wall,
the two walls which encompassed a square enclosure. The artists' efforts to
produce a likeness to real marble tablets apparently succeeded, at least to
the extent of convincing Josephus, who recorded, as we have seen, that the
walls of the building were panelled in that material.

The artists also succeeded with another item in 'taking in' visitors,
including Josephus, who wrote that each pillar was made of a single stone.
We found that this was not so. The pillars were constructed of several drums
of soft stone, plastered and then grooved giving them the appearance of
giant sculptured monolithic columns. Crowning them were Corinthian
capitals, and these, too, were painted. We were fortunate to discover one
of these capitals. It was well preserved and still retained its original covering
of gold paint.

This terrace had not been constructed to hold the main living quarters. *The terrace was for*
The tremendous energies invested in its engineering were designed to serve *rest and relaxation*
the single purpose of creating a magnificent and decorative edifice to be
used for rest and relaxation, for leisure and pleasure, a place from which
one could enjoy the wondrous scenery northwards to Ein Gedi and beyond,
eastwards across the Dead Sea to the mountains of Moab, westwards to the
hills of Judea. This feature was very evident, particularly in the light of a
unique discovery which was quite astonishing. We were removing the large
mounds of debris which covered the eastern side of the terrace, and we had
just begun to clear the subterranean rooms which had already been
spotted in the 1955–6 survey and thought then to be, and so described as,
storerooms. It suddenly became clear that here, on the slope of the steep
rock some 1,100 feet above the Dead Sea, Herod had built a private bath-
house designed in the finest tradition of Roman baths: a cold water pool; a
tepid room; and a hot room with an installation for warming the air – a
double floor, the upper one supported by pillars. Some of these pillars were
still standing. (We shall elaborate on this system of heating when we
describe the large bath-house built by Herod just south of this palace.)
This completed the architectural plan of the lower terrace. Here Herod
could enjoy his leisure with his companions, refreshing himself in the small
bath-house, and then banqueting and relaxing against the pillars and
decorated walls while he took in the impressive view.

The wall paintings and other architectural features of this terrace were
preserved throughout the last 2,000 years because they were covered by
debris, and also because of the dry climate generally prevailing at Masada.
We, however, were now faced by a grave problem: how were we to protect
these finds against the ravages of nature and human vandalism? During
the months of our excavations, despite the bitter criticism it evoked

A detail showing a stylized palm tree,
a rare representation in this palace.

Overleaf:
A restorer at work
on the frescoes.

Vandalism from visitors who felt an urge to put their names on the antiquities – fortunately the inscription shown here was removable.

Damage by vandalism among the general public, we put the site out of bounds to visitors. We did this for several reasons, the principal one being that we simply did not have the means to provide suitable guides, and we could not leave the finds unguarded. We could not risk exposing them to even the few among the visitors who might not have been educated to a proper respect for sites of antiquity, and who might have found it difficult to repress the urge to immortalise their visit. On 1 May 1964, the very day we left the site on completion of our first season of excavation, a group of labourers arrived at Masada to install facilities for the team of restorers who would be continuing their work throughout the summer months. Our chagrin may be imagined when, on our next visit, we found that some of them had marked their names and the date, in black oil paint, over the ancient wall paintings. These people were clearly unaware that they were doing anything reprehensible, for they would certainly not have added their exact address – as some did. But this very fact was all the more disturbing, and our chief concern was how to ensure against unwitting vandalism in the future. On this occasion the damage was not serious; the paint was still fresh, and a prominent paint manufacturer in the country sent us one of his experts to clean the markings. They were successfully removed.

More serious was the problem of protecting the surface of the walls from the onslaughts of nature. The plaster on which the decorations had been painted had been partially eroded over the centuries. Our first attempts to keep the paintings intact, such as injecting glue by a special needle, proved unsatisfactory. We approached the UNESCO department for the

Treatment with glue for frescoes of the lower terrace by a Dutch volunteer.

'First-aid' to frescoes: a restorer injects glue into the plaster.

Technique for preserving the paintings

preservation of historical sites, located in Rome, and we also sought the advice of Italian experts, and they recommended a process, also followed in Italy, which was felt to be the only one which would suit our circumstances. This method entailed removing the paintings, scraping off most of the plaster and leaving them with an original plaster backing of only about one millimetre in thickness, then applying a new and strengthened backing, placing each painting in a special frame, and restoring the framed paintings to their original places.

The task was complicated and costly, but many of the wall paintings seen on the site by visitors today were subjected to this process, and, as a result, we hope they will long be preserved. It would of course have been easier to remove them and put them on view in a museum. But we felt that the wall paintings of Masada should be seen in their original location.

Above: A tense moment when a fresco is detached from the wall for treatment. After removing salt and deteriorated plaster from the back, the frescoes are re-installed in special frames. The restorer on the right was an expert in this kind of work from Kashmir. *Opposite:* An Indonesian member of the expedition reinforces plaster from behind with specially prepared mortar.

53

Here, and only here, do they illustrate the grandeur with which Herod invested his magnificent palace.

This, then, was the story of this structure in the days of Herod, a story of sumptuous luxury. We turn now to the other way of life at Masada, the remains unearthed in our excavations belonging to the period of the Great Jewish Revolt. The contrast was dramatic – more on this site than on any other – between the opulence of the Herodian finds and the poverty of the remains from the days of the revolt. But those were days of spiritual nobility, and this touched us more than all the physical luxury of Herod.

After we had removed the upper layers of debris, but before we had completely uncovered the level containing the wall paintings, we came across a thick layer of ashes, the product of a powerful fire, in which we found remains of food, such as date and olive stones, and also coins struck during the revolt, with such typical inscriptions as: 'The Freedom of Zion'. It was clear that we were bringing to light the remains of that very fire mentioned by Josephus when he recorded that the fighters of Masada burned their communal buildings before they took their lives, to prevent their being used by the Roman conquerors.

Discovery of the remains of the last defenders of Masada

When, however, we came to clear the formidable pile of debris which covered the chambers of the small bath-house, we were arrested by a find which it is difficult to consider in archaeological terms, for such an experience is not normal in archaeological excavations. Even the veterans and the more cynical among us stood frozen, gazing in awe at what had been uncovered; for as we gazed, we relived the final and most tragic moments of the drama of Masada. Upon the steps leading to the cold-water pool and on the ground nearby were the remains of three skeletons. One was that of a man of about twenty – perhaps one of the commanders of Masada. Next to it we found hundreds of silvered scales of armour, scores of arrows, fragments of a prayer shawl (*talith*), and also an ostracon (an inscribed potsherd) with Hebrew letters. Not far off, also on the steps, was the skeleton of a young woman, with her scalp preserved intact because of the extreme dryness of the atmosphere. Her dark hair, beautifully plaited, looked as if it had just been freshly coiffeured. Next to it the plaster was stained with what looked like blood. By her side were delicately fashioned lady's sandals, styled in the traditional pattern of the period. The third skeleton was that of a child. There could be no doubt that what our eyes beheld were the remains of some of the defenders of Masada. In describing the last moments, Josephus writes:

And he who was the last of all, took a view of all the other bodies lest perchance some or other among so many that were slain, should want his assistance to be quite despatched; and when he perceived that they were all slain, he set fire to the palace, and with the force of his hand ran his sword entirely through himself, and fell down dead near to his own relations.

Could it be that we had discovered the bones of that very fighter and of his kith? This, of course, we can never know for certain.

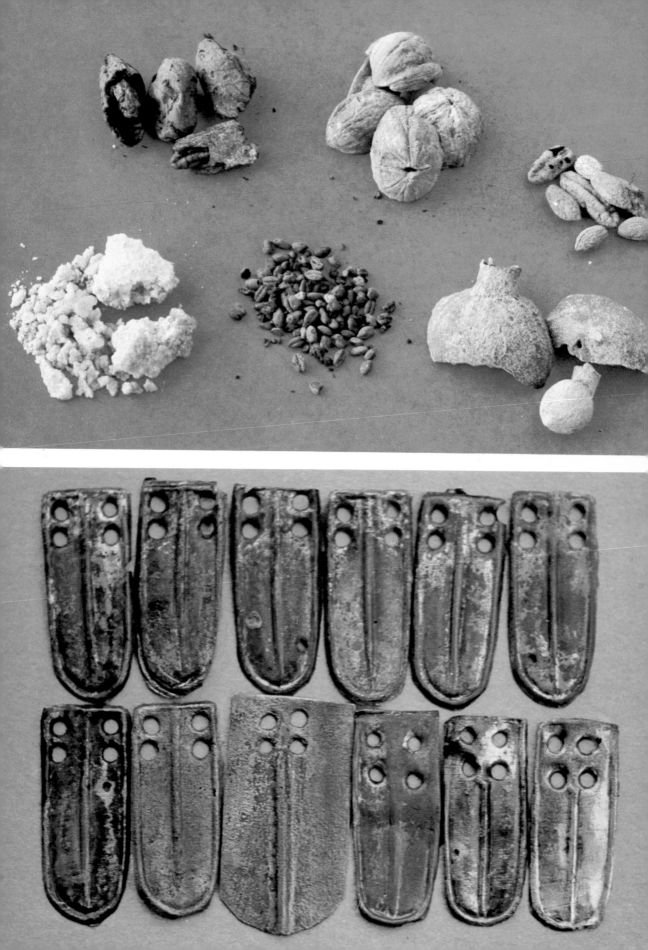

Leather sandals found near the skeleton of a woman, startlingly modern in design.

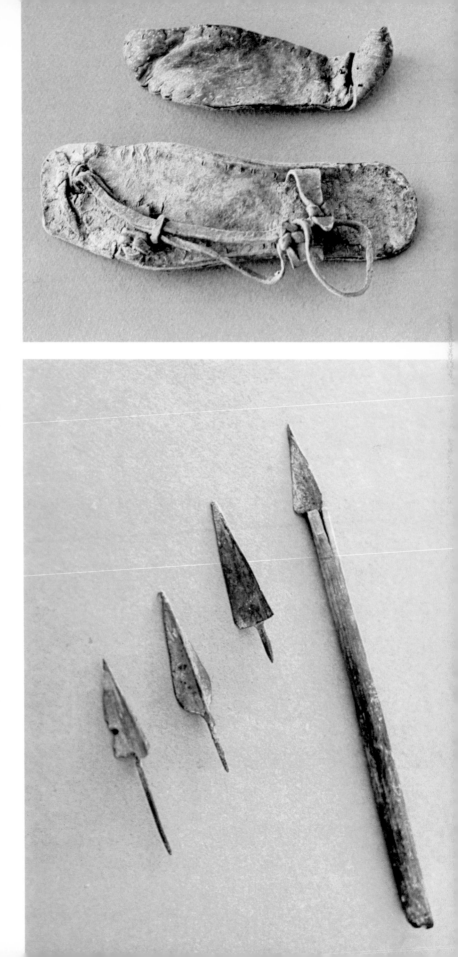

Left: One of the most amazing finds was this plaited hair still attached to the scalp of a young woman, whose skeleton was near that of the warrior and the child.

Scores of iron arrows were also found near the Zealot warrior. One arrow still has its original wooden shaft.

The middle terrace

The middle terrace remained something of a mystery up to the time of our excavation. Even before we started digging the only thing discernible on this terrace was a circular structure. The bulk of it had been uncovered during the 1955–6 survey, and what then lay revealed were two concentric walls, the space between them containing fragments of capitals and drums which had fallen into it. The tops of the walls had been smoothly levelled, and it was evident that this was the foundation for a columned structure. These two round walls, and particularly the empty space between them, *The nature of the* prompted much speculation, and various theories had been presented to *circular structure* explain their use; but none was satisfactory. When we started our work,

A view of the rear structure of the middle terrace: on the right a hidden staircase leads to the upper terrace.

these walls, as I have said, had already been uncovered, and what we therefore did was to concentrate largely on the area to the immediate south, literally beneath the rock of the upper terrace. During the 1955–6 survey the teams had come across square pillars attached to the wall with niches between them, and it had then been suggested that perhaps this was a place of worship and the recesses had held statues.

Excavation of this site was not easy. It was heaped with huge rocks, some weighing hundreds of pounds, which, throughout the ages, had fallen from the upper terrace. The work at this stage of the dig was a sheer physical grind. But when we had cleared the whole area, it was apparent that here was a space which had originally been roofed. Running off its eastern and western sides were rooms. Its southern side held several pilasters which had partially supported the roof.

Today we are confident that the entire structure on this central terrace was designed in fact to serve only the purposes of leisure and relaxation, like the lower terrace. The architectural pattern was similar to that of many other structures that were popular at the time in the Hellenistic world, as may be seen from the wall paintings at Pompeii, or the face of the tombs at Petra. The circular building may have had two rows of pillars supporting the roof, and the floor, probably of wood, rested on the two concentric walls which served as a base for the columns. South of this building was an area similar to the one we have already described in the lower terrace, a place where one could sit, eat, relax and look at the view.

Structure shown to be area of relaxation

Why the empty space between the two concentric walls? We came upon the secret of this somewhat odd architectural feature when we discovered more of the building methods of Herod's engineers, both in the lower and the upper terraces. They were faced with this problem: since the 'tooth' of rock was extremely narrow at this spot, how were they to construct foundations for the two rows of pillars on the rock itself? The rock was of uneven height, so the foundation walls – particularly the outer one – were of considerable height. The purpose of the empty space between them was to ease the pressure on the outer wall.

Here, too, the lower part of the southern walls of the structure on the middle terrace had once been decorated with paintings, but few remained. On the south-western side, the bottom portion of a staircase was discovered. This part had been built; its upper part had been cut in the rock. There is no doubt that it was to this staircase and to the one leading down to the lower terrace that Josephus was referring when he recorded that Herod built and cut a hidden and invisible staircase. And, indeed, one can walk up or down these stairs from one terrace to the other without being seen from the outside. Unfortunately, most of the upper part of the staircase has long collapsed. But the little that has remained testifies to the skill and daring of Herod's engineers.

Overleaf: Looking down on the middle terrace from the upper terrace.
Roman camp D is in the background about 900 feet below.

The magnificent view from the upper terrace towards Ein-Gedi in the north and the Dead Sea and Moab mountains to the east. Living quarters can be seen at the bottom and a semi-circular porch in the centre. Some of these rooms were added by Byzantine monks.

The upper terrace

Living quarters found on upper terrace

The only area in the entire palace which served as the living quarters proper was the upper terrace. It consisted of two parts. Its northern section was a large semi-circular porch commanding a breath-taking view of the north, the east and the west. It was built with double walls, similar to the concentric walls of the middle terrace. South of this porch were the dwelling chambers. Parts of this area had already been examined during the 1955–6 survey, and the impression had been gained that this section contained many rooms. But our excavations showed that several of the chambers must be ascribed to the work of the Byzantine monks who erected a number of buildings on Masada in the 5th century.

The fact is that in the entire residential area on this terrace, there were no more than four original dwelling rooms and several corridors. It was quite clear that this northern palace, whose construction had demanded such formidable efforts and resources, was not intended to house a large number of people. It had been built for Herod alone, or perhaps for himself and one of his nine wives.

Opposite: Like other Herodian mosaics these mosaic floors in the living quarters on the upper terrace of the villa are among the earliest ever found in the Holy Land. Note the extreme simplicity of the design.

This dwelling area, too, was ornately decorated, possibly more lavishly than the middle and bottom terraces. In some of the rooms we were lucky enough to find mosaic floors still in a reasonable state of preservation. In one, for example, we came across a floor of white mosaic stones bearing a simple geometric pattern of hexagons in black stone. This mosaic, like other Herodian mosaic floors, is among the oldest to be discovered so far in this country. The other Herodian mosaics, which we shall have occasion to see later, are done in more than two colours, and are much more ornate, and seem to have been intended to impress the visitor. Here, the aim was simplicity.

The walls and ceilings of the rooms were of course adorned with paintings; but the buildings on this terrace had been looted and damaged by the successive conquerors and occupiers – the Zealots, the Roman victors and the Byzantine monks – so that it was only here and there that we found a fairly undisturbed section which testified to the opulent decor which once graced this portion of the palace.

Actually, the little we were able to learn of the original architectural embellishments of this upper terrace stemmed from what we found not on the site of the palace itself but in the area slightly to its south.

Even before we began our excavations, one could see here what looked like a huge embankment of earth, its slope running down from north to south. Emerging from its ridge were several stones, suggesting that these formed the top of a wall or barrier running from east to west which

Many finds produced by sieving excavated earth

separated the palace from the rest of Masada. This detail, too, accords with the descriptions of Josephus. From the very outset, therefore, we assigned a team of *Gadna* to excavate this huge pile of earth. As we had done with all locations of the dig, here, too, every grain of earth that was removed was put through a special sieve, which was an innovation in excavation technique in this country. Close to 50,000 cubic yards of Masada earth were sifted during the course of the archaeological dig. This method slowed up the pace of the work, but it proved itself in results. For it was precisely among what was left behind on the sieves that we found hundreds of coins, scores of inscriptions on pottery and tiny items like jewellery which are easy to miss.

The youngsters of *Gadna* who were working in this location, each group doing a fortnightly stint, had long had the feeling that their work was pretty futile. Nothing impressive had been discovered in this earth pile, and so disappointed were they that the wall that was being uncovered was dubbed by them 'the Wailing Wall of the *Gadna*'. But in fact they had not toiled in vain. After eleven months of excavation, the wall stood revealed – a great wall with white plaster belonging to the Herodian period and in an

'Gadna' youth corps volunteers sifting and digging the enormous pile of earth covering the great plastered wall separating the villa from the rest of Masada.

64

extraordinarily fine state of preservation, a Masada landmark visible today from far off. Of much greater importance, however, were the numerous objects found by the *Gadna* teams amid the dumped rubble, objects which had been flung from the palace and the neighbouring area during the period of the Zealots, the Roman garrison and the Byzantine occupiers. Thus we found here a great many sherds of handsome pottery vessels of eastern *terra sigillata* type, which assuredly at one time had adorned the palace. Also found were many pieces of painted plaster which must have graced the ceilings and walls all over the upper terrace. They were unmatched in excellence by anything that had come to light on the bottom terrace, or indeed in any other location on Masada.

The biggest surprise of all, however, were the architectural finds. In and around these heaps of earth and rubble we discovered scores of pillar drums, as well as bases and capitals, which had been flung higgledy-piggledy in the dump. This offered evidence that there were pillars on the upper terrace, too, and also that these were not made of a single stone, but of several stone sections.

Two Scandinavian members of the expedition
reinforcing Herodian plaster on a hot day.

Above: Two eastern 'terra sigillata' platters salvaged from the debris covering the plastered wall.

Right: Fragment of painted plaster which proves that the rooms in the upper terrace were decorated with frescoes.

Below: Many of the architectural elements from the upper terrace were found in the heap of debris covering the plastered wall. The bases, drums and capitals of the columns are of particular interest.

The masons marked each column with a letter and each drum with a number. Here is drum 1 of column T, marked by the Hebrew letter 'Tet', evidence that the builders and stone masons were Jewish.

A capital bearing the Hebrew letter 'Qof' (Q).

Drum 4 of column 'Mem' (M).

Since there were a number of columns and each consisted of several drums, the ancient masons and builders had to put a working mark on each drum so that it could be put into its proper place, fitting snugly between its neighbours, when the assembly stage was reached. They would assign a letter to the column and a number to the drum. To our surprise, the letters used by the masons were Hebrew letters, inscribed on the stone with a faithful hand, and at the side of each was a number indicating the position of the drum. This shows clearly that the builders and stone-masons were Jewish. These markings were working aids only; they would not be seen once the pillars were assembled and the building was completed.

Discovery of Jewish stone-masons' working marks

At one spot we found the components of column T – the Hebrew letter *Tet* – and in the picture we can see the drum marked *Tet*. At another spot we found a capital bearing the Hebrew letter *Qof*, while close to the upper terrace we unearthed sections of other pillars. Particularly beautiful are the inscriptions of the Hebrew letter *Mem* – M. We have today sections bearing the mark of most of the letters of the alphabet. Actually, the number of pillars in the upper terrace and in buildings elsewhere in the palace area was greater than the number of letters in the alphabet, and the builders, we found, had recourse to signs outside the regular alphabet. Some stones were marked with letters in Paleo-Hebrew script. On the bottom terrace some pillars bore markings of Latin letters, others of geometric signs. They had apparently run out of letters for marking columns. Incidentally, in the light of our finds, we would hazard a guess that the pillars on the upper terrace were used to beautify the impressive semi-circular balcony.

One of the problems on which we spent much time and effort was concerned with the original entry to the complex of palace terraces. The large wall effectively, and intentionally, sealed approaches to the palace, leaving only a narrow passage-way at its eastern end. At this spot an opening was discovered during the 1955–6 survey, and next to it a bench. We concentrated our excavations in this sector in the hope that we would bring to light the staircase system leading from the rest of the Masada summit to this entrance, and indeed we were successful, finding a set of broad steps comfortable to negotiate.

Excavation of staircases revealed two stages of building

While digging, we discovered beneath this set of steps the remains of an earlier staircase, clear evidence of an earlier stage in the building of the palace. As a matter of fact we have much proof, both in this location and in the area of the large wall, that there were two building stages. The question of course is whether the first stage pre-dated Herod and must be ascribed to the work of 'Jonathan the High Priest', or whether both stages took place during the Herodian period. The problem is complicated, but I would venture to suggest that both stages belong to the period of Herod. To my mind, after he had started building (stage one), structural changes (stage two) were introduced, both as a result of changes in the architectural plan during the course of construction, which certainly took a number of years, and also following the great earthquake which we know occurred during the reign of Herod.

In our efforts to uncover and bring to light this staircase system, we were forced to excavate the eastern sector, working literally on the edge of the perpendicular rock which hangs 1,300 feet above the level of the Dead Sea.

The volunteers who worked here had to be attached to rope belts so that they could operate in safety, just as did other teams working in other dangerous sectors of the summit perimeter. The excavation here revealed additional architectural remains belonging to the upper terrace, among them handsome capitals, this time of Ionic style, in contrast to the Corinthian capitals on the pillars of the lower terrace. We also found here the ruins of a small bath-house. The construction of this, too, had been interrupted in the course of the building, and there is the same uncertainty about its date as there is about the other structures mentioned above.

Palace referred to by Josephus not the main Herodian palace

With the completion of our excavations, we now have a comprehensive picture of the plan and grandeur of the magnificent palace built by Herod at the northern edge of the rock of Masada, so elaborately described by Josephus. But today we can say with certainty that even though this is the palace referred to in the writings of Josephus, it is not the main Masada palace of Herod, the ceremonial, administrative and official palace of the king. This latter palace we discovered in another sector, at the western edge of the summit, and this was the very building which former scholars had erroneously taken to be the palace described by Josephus.

Above: An Ionic capital discovered in the debris of the upper terrace.
Opposite: Equally attractive is this Corinthian capital found on the lower terrace of the palace-villa.

Work on the cliff included the dangers of mountaineering.

Today, I think, we can term it the northern palace, to distinguish it from the large western palace, the royal palace-villa. For, despite the wealth of effort, ingenuity and resources poured into this elaborate structure, it had dwelling quarters only on the upper terrace, and even here there were only a few living rooms. Why did Herod build this villa in so isolated a spot, on a difficult site which posed such an architectural and engineering challenge? Why did he choose a location which demanded the complicated construction of support walls before he could even start building the palace?

This is the highest point on Masada, and it thus commands the best view of the surrounding countryside and has a natural defence advantage. Moreover, it is close to the lower water cisterns and the path leading to them. However, it seems to me that the principal and determining factor in Herod's choice of this location was climate. The eleven months that we spent on Masada familiarised us with its two climatic problems: the sun that sears throughout most of the year; and the raging south wind. The northern point of the Masada rock – particularly the middle and bottom terraces – is the only site on Masada which is sheltered for most of the day-light hours: sheltered from the sun, so that it is cool and pleasant, and sheltered from the south wind – the rock walls of each terrace serve as wind-breaks – so that it is always still.

Only Herod, the great and ambitious builder, could have conceived the project for erecting a three-tiered hanging palace-villa for himself on this spot.

Opposite: This aerial view from the north, on completion of the dig, makes clear the relation of the three terraces of the palace-villa.

6 The large bath-house

Emerging from the ground in the area to the immediate south of the upper terrace and west of the complex of storehouses were parts of the ruins of a large building. These were always visible to visitors to Masada. Particularly conspicuous was what looked like a large hall, thirty-three by thirty-six feet, with walls six feet thick.

Because of its location and the thickness of its walls, this structure had been thought by various scholars to have been a defence tower for the protection of the storehouses and the approach to the northern palace-villa. Other scholars held it to have been the centre from which the storehouses were administered. We thought so, too, as we approached our task of clearing the huge mounds of debris which covered it. But the excavations produced a great surprise. Soon after we had started removing the rubble from the large hall, we uncovered the walls and found them plastered. In the plaster were impressions of clay piping. It was not difficult to guess that what we were clearing was the hot room (*caldarium*) of a large bath-house in the Roman style. As we dug deeper, we found that there were pipes of clay, to carry the heat, in all the walls. Amid the debris, too, we came across many such pipes, rectangular in cross-section.

Excavation of the large bath-house

The decisive proof, however, that we were in the *caldarium* appeared when we had excavated down to the fragment of a floor. Beneath it was another floor, and between the two we discovered more than 200 tiny pillars, most of them made of round clay bricks which were beautifully preserved, as customarily found in the hypocaust, the underground heating chamber of the *caldarium*.

The walls were faced with perpendicular clay pipes which ran right to the bottom floor. Adjacent to the building was an oven from which the hot air issued into the space between the two floors of the *caldarium*, and from there, through the wall pipes, into the hot room itself. This room was almost without any opening, and it was possible to heat it to high temperatures. Then by pouring water on the hot floor, it became a steam bath.

All the parts of the installations connected with this hot room were

Opposite above: The ruins of the large bath-house before excavation; on the left the thick walls of the *caldarium*, and right and top the ruins of the storeroom and the administrative building before excavation. *Opposite below:* Hot room (*caldarium*) during the dig. The impressions of clay pipes are clearly visible on the wall plaster.
Overleaf: View from the south of the *caldarium* on completion of excavation. The tiny pillars, made mostly of round clay bricks, supported the upper floor of which only a fragment still exists. The entrance to the tepid room is on the left. Compare with the picture on page 80.

extremely well-preserved, and what we had excavated turned out to be one of the most beautiful and complete examples of a Roman bath-house, among the most ancient ever discovered in the country and the region.

In a corner of the hot room we found a few pipes still stuck to the wall. A small portion of the upper floor was also found in its original place, still supported by small pillars. Examination of the pipes showed that they also had holes in the sides, all the way up so that the hot air issued not only from the top end of the pipe but also from these holes.

The bath-house compared with those of Jericho and Herodion

Against the northern side of the *caldarium* was a semi-circular niche in which once stood a huge tub made of quartz. (We found many fragments of this.) Water was brought to the tub from the outside through a lead pipe under considerable pressure, so that it squirted up like a fountain. (Parts of the lead pipe were also discovered.) On the other side of the room was a rectangular cell and in it we found the remains of the bath which had originally been used for hot water. This arrangement, both in its plan and technical details, is not only identical with that of other bath-houses (less well-preserved) of the Herodian period discovered both at Jericho and Herodion, but is almost exactly like the handsome Roman bath-houses of Pompeii and Herculaneum. The upper floor was paved in a geometric design of alternating black and white tiles.

In the course of our excavations here we discovered that in the first

The tepid room and its frescoes. Impressions of the black and white tiles which decorated the room are also visible.

A closer view of the frescoes in the tepid room shows
their similarity to those of the lower terrace.

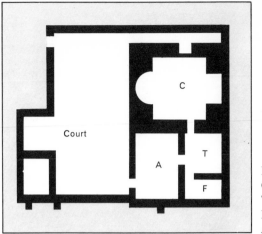

Plan of bath-house.
C = *caldarium*
T = *tepidarium*
F = *frigidarium*
A = *apoditerium*

stage of building there was a mosaic floor which was later changed for this paved floor. We found that the same thing had occurred in the other rooms of the bath-house. It may be assumed that this change is of the same order and was due to the same causes as the structural changes which we discussed earlier. It is possible that the mosaic floor collapsed during the great earthquake, and was later replaced by a paved floor of the type known in Latin as *opus sectile*.

When it became clear to us that the large hall was not a defence tower nor an administrative building but the *caldarium* of a bath-house, it was evident that the adjoining rooms on the west could be none other than the customary additional rooms of the standard Roman bath-house, namely, the cold room (*frigidarium*), tepid room (*tepidarium*), and entrance and disrobing room (*apoditerium*).

And, indeed, a glance at the plan and at the air photograph shows that our bath-house was built to this pattern. The small room was the *frigidarium*, and it was strictly functional, designed for speedy entry into the cold water and speedy exit therefrom. It is for this reason that it was built on austere lines. This chamber was discovered in a very good state of preservation, and it is really nothing more than a pool similar to other pools and cisterns found at Masada and elsewhere, with steps running from top to bottom with water-proof plaster to prevent seepage.

Between the cold room and the hot room lay the tepid room. This, unlike the *frigidarium*, was a luxuriously built chamber, done in the rich style of the northern palace-villa. Its walls were decorated with paintings which followed the villa pattern, and its floor was paved with black and white tiles as in the hot room, though they were smaller. Unfortunately, however, most of these had been torn from their original place and were not even to be found among the debris. We did manage to unearth a few, but most of these were broken. We had the same experience with the *apoditerium*. It seems probable that the Roman garrison, before leaving Masada, pulled out the expensive tiles and took them off, either to sell

Opposite: The pipes for hot air circulation are still fixed to the wall of the south-east corner of the *caldarium*.

81

This fragment of a carved lintel from the bath-house court was
re-used by the Zealots for building material.

Opposite above: In the north-east corner of the *apoditerium* the lower
parts of the original frescoes have been covered by a tiny bathing
pool added either by the Zealots or the Roman garrison.
Opposite below: Fragments of the painted plaster ceiling of the
apoditerium as they were found.

them or to use them in their next posting. The *apoditerium* was also large and lavishly built. It had wall paintings, as in the *tepidarium*, and a paved floor with black and white triangular tiles. The ceiling of this disrobing room had also been decorated with paintings. It had collapsed long ago, and we found fragments of the painted plaster on the floor, the colouring and the style of execution showing considerable artistry. (It may be assumed that the ceilings in the other rooms had been similarly decorated.) These paintings in the *apoditerium* were different from those in the palace-villa, with their schematic style and attempted imitation of marble

A section of the mosaic floor of the bathroom court. The execution and the design are identical with the mosaic floor of the upper terrace (see page 63).

panels. The ceiling in the *apoditerium* combined a geometric and floral design.

Additional structural changes in this bath-house were introduced after the capture of Masada by the Zealots, and further changes were made by the Roman garrison who occupied this site for several decades after their victory in 73 A.D. This explains the various additions we found, particularly in the *apoditerium*. In the north-eastern corner of this chamber we discovered a small reservoir, rather like a tiny bathing pool. It had obviously been built later than the bath-house, for not only did it stand on the original paving tiles, but its walls crudely covered part of the original wall-paintings. Similarly, our excavations brought to light a bench built against the walls, also covering the original plaster and resting on the original paved floor. It had been made of re-used drums of Herodian pillars. These additions and alterations had been carried out partly by the Zealots and partly by the Roman garrison.

Structural changes in the bath-house

At the entrance to the bath-house there was a wide courtyard through which one also reached (from the east) the heating installations. As we unearthed it, we found this court much destroyed, but the few remains showed it to have been handsomely built. Its floor had originally been a mosaic, and parts of it were still preserved. This mosaic was identical with the mosaics we found on the upper terrace of the palace, both in colour – black and white – and in design. The special importance of this fact lies in its proof that the bath-house and at least the upper terrace were built during the same stage of construction, and its paintings and mosaics were executed by the same artists.

Running around the eastern, northern and western sides of the court was roofing which rested on pillars. Only near the entrance to the tepid room did we find the pillars still in their original position, and we saw that their capitals were of Nabatean style. Between the tops of the pillars and the roof had run the lintel, decorated with metopes bearing rosettes. We found sections of this lintel scattered in several places. They had also been used by the Zealots or the Roman troops to repair the oven of the baths. This is a good example of what has frequently happened in many ages – where the architectural ornaments of one period were later used as common building materials without any relation to their decorative feature. The picture on page 83 also illustrates the material decline of Masada at the time of the Zealots and during the period of the occupying Roman garrison.

As the plan shows, the bath-house was built in line with the upper terrace, and there is no doubt that it formed part of the complex of handsome buildings which Herod erected here for himself and his family, as well as for the garrison he had with him. This bath-house, like other water systems we shall describe later, is of special significance, standing as it does on the summit of dry and arid Masada, and requiring vast efforts to keep it supplied with water. But then Masada was not an ordinary fort but a royal citadel. Nothing was spared to enable the king and his companions to live there, in the desert, and still enjoy their customary amenities.

Further evidence of importance of site as a royal citadel

An aerial view from the north of the storehouse complex before excavation, showing how the layout of the area was clear before digging. The large bath-house is in the centre and the administrative building on the right. A closer view of the storerooms before excavation is on pages 92 and 93.

86

7 The storehouses

The large rectangular structures in the north-east section of Masada, just south of the palace-villa, have been accepted by most scholars as the storehouses built by Herod, and are thus described by Josephus:

As for the furniture that was within this fortress, it was still more wonderful on account of its splendour and long continuance; for here was laid up corn in large quantities, and such as would subsist men for a long time; here was also wine and oil in abundance with all kinds of pulse and dates heaped up together; all which Eleazar found there, when he and his Sicarii got possession of the fortress by treachery. These fruits were also fresh and full ripe, and no way inferior to such fruits newly laid in, although they were little short of a hundred years from the laying in of these provisions. Till the place was taken by the Romans; nay, indeed, when the Romans got possession of those fruits that were left, they found them not corrupted all that while: nor should we be mistaken, if supposed that the air was here the cause of their enduring so long, this fortress being so high, and so free from the mixture of all terrene and muddy particles of matter. There was also found here a large quantity of all sorts of weapons of war, which had been treasured up by that king, and were sufficient for ten thousand men; there was cast-iron and brass and tin which shew that he had taken much pains to have all things here ready for the greatest occasions.

It was easy to identify the remains of these buildings, for their architectural plan was typical of storehouse construction throughout the ages, namely, long narrow halls, almost without openings.

The storerooms of Masada were built in two main groups: the southern group, the larger of the two, and the second, just to the east of the bathhouse. The two blocks of storehouses were separated by a road which ran from east to west. When we came to excavate these buildings, we were faced with a tough problem, which was also to crop up with the unearthing of other structures: they were in a state of almost complete destruction.

Excavation of storehouses

It is true that the lines of the storeroom walls show up well in the air photograph, which was taken before the excavations; but these lines mark only the stumps of the ruined walls. The main parts of the walls and the roofs had long fallen in, the result both of the destruction of the site by the Zealots and of the series of earthquakes which hit the region in later years. There were instances where the stones of a wall collapsed a row at a time, an entire layer falling in one spot, as may be seen in the picture on page 92.

The storehouses, like the other buildings at Masada, were built of hard dolomite stone quarried on the site. Because of its toughness, the stone was not dressed to a fine smoothness, the masons satisfying themselves with the coarse fashioning of corners on each slab sufficient to enable them to be used for building. The walls were built up of double rows of these stone slabs, so that the thickness of a wall was double the width of a slab. The slabs themselves were large, each weighing from 400 to 500 lbs.

Storehouses restored first, excavated afterwards

How were we to excavate such a formidable set of buildings strewn with thousands of its fallen stones? If this had been an ordinary archaeological site we would no doubt have tried to roll the stones to the edge of the plateau, dropped them over the precipice, and applied ourselves without further delay to the task of digging. But Masada is no ordinary site, and we had to concern ourselves not only with our own immediate expedition but with the future – with the hundreds of thousands of visitors drawn by the drama of Masada, who would wish to see something of the physical remains of Masada's past. We accordingly decided on a procedure quite different from that customarily followed in an archaeological excavation. In co-operation with the Department for the Preservation of Historic Sites in the Israeli Prime Minister's Office, we decided to undertake the restoration of the storehouses first, and to dig afterwards. In other words, what we did was to pick up all the stones scattered on the ground and use them to restore the walls, assembling them layer by layer upon the sections of ruined walls that still stood. Then with the ground thus cleared, we could start excavating. We did not imagine we could restore each stone to its original position, but I can say that we were sufficiently careful to ensure that each was replaced in the original wall from which it had fallen. And, indeed, when our task was completed, with not a slab left on the ground, it transpired that the original height of all the walls of all the storerooms had been the same – about eleven feet.

This system, which seemed to us appropriate and which worked out so successfully, was easier to plan than to implement. We needed expert builders, and we also needed to haul up to Masada cranes to clear the stones and hoist them into position. Fortunately we had with us Moshe Yoffe, the veteran mason who has had a hand in the restoration of many historical sites in Israel. The cranes had to be of the manual kind, with tripod, pulley and chain, so that Masada at times looked more like an oil-drilling area than an archaeological excavation site.

Incidentally, in order that the future visitor should be able to tell which part of the wall was still standing when we unearthed it and which had been restored, we painted a black line between the two. It was just as well that we did so while the restored wall was being built up, for Moshe Yoffe and his men were so skilled that at times we ourselves found it difficult to determine where the work of Herod's builders stopped and that of Yoffe began. Actually, in most of the buildings we did not restore the walls to their original height but only up to three, six or nine feet, as we thought fit, and I think we managed to preserve its character as an ancient site.

Left: One of the cranes specially devised for lifting stones for restoration was of the same basic construction as the Roman cranes most probably used by Herod.

Below left: A drawing of a Roman crane of the type most probably used by Herod's builders.

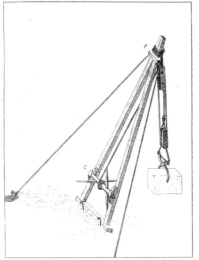

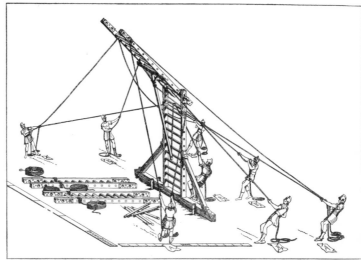

Left: The expedition once more followed Herod's example in erecting this tripod for a crane.

Above: A drawing of the erection of a similar Roman contrivance.

89

The task of removing some of the boulders and debris required the use of mechanical equipment, such as tractors, which of course could not be driven up to the summit. What we had to do was take them apart, send each section to the top by an overhead cable rail which was installed by the army engineers, and then assemble the parts.

To return to the storehouses, in the photograph opposite one can see the parallel layers of stones as they fell during the earthquake. A typical group of storerooms as they look after restoration and after excavation can be seen in the bottom pictures. We excavated numerous storerooms, but not all. Nor did we restore all. This was intentional. We decided to leave some as we found them before the dig so that visitors may see what they looked like, and, by contrasting them with the others, gain an impression of the work of excavation and of restoration.

In several of them, after we had cleared stone and debris up to a depth

A section of the storeroom after excavation and reconstruction, seen from the south. The white plastered wall at the top belongs to the palace-villa.

One of the store-
rooms before
excavation (looking
north).

The same storeroom after excavation and reconstruction.
In the foreground are traces of ash and broken pottery.

The stones of the collapsed walls lying in rows on the floor as the result of an earthquake are clearly visible in this closer view of the storerooms before excavation. The *caldarium* of the large bath-house (before excavation) is on the right.

92

Storage jars after restoration. These and others are very important archaeologically since they can be dated with certainty between Herod's time and 73 AD. Some bore Hebrew inscriptions indicating their owners' names.

Charred beams lying on the
floor of one of the storerooms
as a result of the great fire of
the Zealots. The pierced object
was probably a mould; it lies
as found.

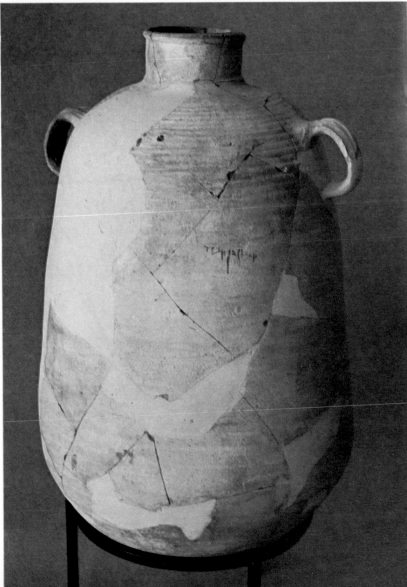

Left: Jar on which the name
'Shimeon ben Yoezer' is
inscribed in ink. The owner
most probably belonged to a
priestly family. *Above:* The
inscription in detail; it
is written in the semicursive
Hebrew square script.

of three or more feet, we reached the level closest to the original floor, and as we did so we beheld an unusual sight of destruction. The whole area was covered with a thick layer of ashes and charred beams, while scattered among them were hundreds of shattered vessels. It was evident that the vessels had not been broken by the falling beams when the roof collapsed in the big fire started by the Zealots, but had been intentionally smashed, to prevent them from falling into the hands of the Romans.

These vessels themselves showed how the storage system for victuals was organised – and an excellent system it was, too. Each storeroom held, exclusively, its own type of vessel: oil jars, wine jars, or jars for flour, each indicated by its shape. Though they were broken, this did not matter from the archaeological point of view, for the experts on our team managed to glue most of the pieces together to look as they do in the picture on page 94.

From a study of the shapes it was possible to conclude that many of the vessels belonged to the Herodian period, but in their final days they had been used by new owners, namely the Jewish defenders of Masada. For they bore inscriptions, in ink and charcoal, of such names as *Shmuel ben Ezra* (Hebrew for 'Samuel, son of Ezra') . . . *Shimeon ben Yoezer* and others.

Pottery with Hebrew inscriptions

Moreover, several of the vessels also carried the Hebrew letter 't' (*Tav* in Hebrew), written in ink and charcoal, and there is no doubt that this stood for the Hebrew word *Truma* – priestly due – as explained in the *Mishna* (the codification of traditional Jewish jurisprudence). These inscriptions, and the inscription *Ma'aser Kohen* (priestly tithe) found in another building, led us to the conclusion that the defenders of Masada were not only Zealots from the national-political point of view but also lived rigidly according to the religious code, strictly adhering to such commandments as tithing, despite the harsh conditions of life at Masada. This characteristic of the

Broken oil and wine storage jars as they were found.
This storeroom contained only jars of this type.

Jewish defenders is also seen in other finds and in other buildings which we shall be describing later.

What we unearthed in the storerooms testified to both planned and sudden destruction. Together with the evidence of the fire and the smashed vessels, we found, for example, in the entrance to one of the chambers, nearly a hundred coins strewn on the floor within a small radius. They belonged to the year two and the year three of the Jewish revolt. It seemed as though the person in charge of the stores, in the final bitter moment, had taken his stock of coins from the treasury and flung them on the floor as useless objects.

Incidentally, the finds of large collections of coins in the public buildings of Masada, such as the storehouses, the bath-house, the ritual baths (*mikve*) and bakeries, point to the pattern of life in the beleaguered fort. It is likely that these coins, which of course had lost their practical value during the siege, may have served as tokens in the hands of the Masada commanders for the rationing of food and services.

In one of the storerooms we also found stocks of tin and other metals, as mentioned by Josephus. On the other hand, we came across a few storerooms which were completely empty, with no vessels and no sign of fire. This raises an interesting problem. Josephus records that according to the decision of Eleazar ben Ya'ir, the stores of victuals were not burned so as to show the Romans that the defenders of Masada died by their own free choice and not through lack of food.

The fact that we found storerooms containing wine, oil and flour jars which were broken and burned might suggest a contradiction to the words of Josephus. But our discovery of empty and unfired storerooms perhaps explains his report, or the report that was transmitted to him, in this way: in order to achieve their purpose, the Zealots did not need to leave *all* their stores of food to the Romans. It was enough for them to leave one or two rooms with untouched victuals to show that they had not died through lack of food. It is possible that the undamaged storerooms which we unearthed were the very rooms in which the Zealots had left food, which was later eaten by the Roman garrison.

Undamaged but empty storerooms found

In none of the storehouses did we find any weapons of war. This too is understandable. The considerable stores of arms which Herod had left at Masada had long been taken out and put to use by Menahem, the first conqueror of Masada. According to Josephus, Menahem had used the weapons he found there in his march on Jerusalem. It may also be assumed that the Roman garrison, and certainly the Zealots during their war, had removed from the stores all the weapons they had found – if indeed any were still there – for their own battle.

The weapons of the Zealots, who used mainly bows and arrows, were discovered by us in many locations on Masada. We found hundreds of arrows, in such places as the middle terrace of the palace-villa, the western palace and elsewhere, literally in heaps where they had been piled and intentionally set on fire. Only very few weapons for hand-to-hand fighting,

Some of the hundreds of bronze coins of the Jewish revolt found in
the storerooms and other public buildings. They bear a vine-leaf
design on one side and a chalice on the other; the inscriptions in the
paleo-Hebrew script read 'For the freedom of Zion'.

Opposite: A unique storeroom most probably built to store wine or other liquids.
Note the plastered floors and walls and the round depression in the floor.

like the sword or spear, were found at Masada; the most effective defence weapon on the walls of the summit was of course the bow and arrow.

Several storerooms were no doubt used for stock-piling, perhaps of special liquids. In one of them, for example, after we had cleared the mounds of debris, we brought to light plastered walls and a floor which had three circular pits, also well plastered, at specifically spaced intervals. It is difficult to tell with certainty what was their purpose, but it is possible that this type of storeroom was designed to hold stocks of, say, wine, and the depressions in the floor were to ease the pouring of the liquid from a large to a smaller vessel, or to trap whatever was spilled in the process.

The excavation and restoration of the storehouses required a considerable physical effort, and even though such work covered only some two-thirds of the structures, it occupied – in addition to the restoration team – groups of volunteers averaging sixty to seventy at a time throughout the entire eleven month period of our expedition. For, apart from digging inside the storerooms, we also had to clear and excavate the streets and alleys which separated the storehouses from each other and the whole complex of stores from the other buildings.

We found the main street in the storehouse area covered by great piles of debris, much of which had come from the adjoining building. An example of this problem can be seen in the photograph below: close to the floor, between the heaps of ruins and ashes, may be spotted a jar, absolutely complete, which was miraculously preserved unbroken, though it was beneath a mound of rubble about six feet high.

The effort, however, was most rewarding, for it is now possible to see,

A street between the storehouses in the process of being excavated. A storage-jar was miraculously preserved intact beneath an accumulation of debris and charred beams. *Opposite:* An aerial view of the storeroom complex on completion of the excavations, showing the well-planned layout.

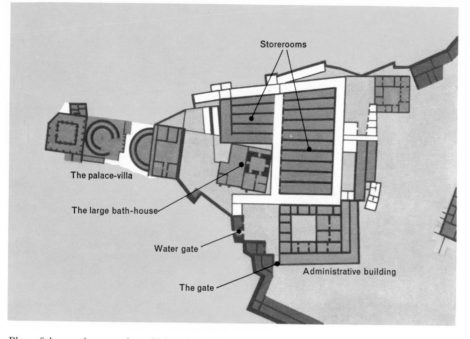

Storerooms

The palace-villa

The large bath-house

Water gate

Administrative building

The gate

Plan of the northern section of Masada, with (left to right)
the palace-villa, the storerooms, the bath-house,
the administrative building and the apartment building.

particularly with the help of the photograph on page 101, the extraordinary plan of the complex of storehouses on whose existence the life of Masada depended. As a matter of fact, at the conclusion of the dig and restoration, we ourselves almost fell victim of the 'trap' built into the carefully planned stores area. When we first reached the site, we could get to the storerooms from all directions, by stepping over the debris that had accumulated against the walls. But when the area was cleared and the restoration completed, we found that it was no longer possible to do this. Access to the storehouses was now possible through one opening alone – at the western corner of the stores compound. Here stood a large rectangular building, which had been erected in Herod's day, containing many rooms round a central court. Our excavation of this building showed that it had served as the administrative centre, close as it was to the most vital site in the area.

We soon discovered that entry to the storehouse compound, the bath-house and the northern palace-villa was possible only through here, and it was clear therefore that there had to be a gate. We decided therefore to dig here, and were rewarded by the revelation of a handsome Herodian gate. This gate led originally to special storerooms surrounding the administrative building, but in the Zealots' time it served as an entrance to the main storehouse complex instead of the older Herodian main gate, which we found in ruins nearby. A single watchman posted here could check all who entered and left this important compound of storehouses, as is well illustrated in the plan above.

*Great effort in
restoration of
storehouse area
rewarded*

Opposite above: Before excavation the layout of the storeroom
indicated the existence of a gate at this spot.
Opposite below: After excavation a handsome gate was revealed in the same
spot with well preserved benches and plaster from the Herodian period.

An aerial view of the
apartment building
before excavation.
The structure in the
middle of the central
court proved after
excavation to be an
addition from the
Byzantine period.

8 The 'apartment' or garrison building

The next ruin we came across as we moved southwards from the store-houses was that of a square building, unique on Masada. Its general outline was apparent even before we started digging, as is evident from the aerial photograph on pages 104–5. This building – and its original purpose – intrigued all the scholars who visited Masada over the last hundred years. The 1955–6 survey team speculated that it probably housed the Roman garrison, and that the structures rising from its large central court may have been associated with Roman worship.

Our excavation of this central court showed that these structures which had been erected upon it belong to a later period – to the Byzantine, in fact. But excavation of the rooms *surrounding* the court produced surprises and important discoveries. A word first about the plan. This building is the only one on Masada which had originally been built as a dwelling place.

Plan of the apartment building. The original Herodian building is indicated in blue, and the Zealots' addition in yellow. Each dwelling unit consists of a large court and two small rooms.

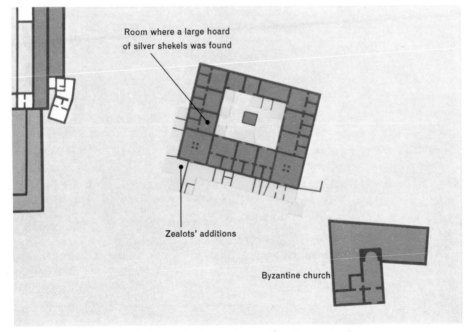

Room where a large hoard of silver shekels was found

Zealots' additions

Byzantine church

Opposite : The apartment building (at bottom) seen from the south after excavation. The structure in the middle of the court is clearly visible.

A shekel and half-shekel after cleaning. *Top:* two faces of a shekel of year 2 with the inscriptions 'Jerusalem the Holy' (*above*) and 'Shekel of Israel' (*below*). *Bottom:* two faces of a half-shekel of year 3 with the inscription 'Jerusalem the Holy' (*above*) and 'Half a shekel' (*below*).

This is clear from the number of identical living quarters which were built around the central court. Each dwelling unit comprised a large room and closed court, and two small adjoining rooms. There can be little doubt that in the days of Herod, this building housed the top administrators of Masada, or perhaps officials, or even garrison troops. But of greater interest was the fact, which became clear during our dig, that in the period of the Jewish revolt some of the most important leaders lived here. This conclusion is based not on the numerous alabaster vessels and handsome cosmetic appurtenances we found in several of the rooms, but on an exciting find in the north-west wing of the building.

I well recall one morning when I was crossing the summit and I became aware of unusual movement in this particular excavation area. When I drew near I saw that the whole group of volunteers assigned to this site were staring fascinated at the floor of the large room of this dwelling unit. There, beneath the level of the original floor, lay a heap of coins stuck together, and from the colour of the mould clinging to them it was clear that these were coins of silver. Bits of cloth were still stuck to part of the heap and it was evident that the coins had originally been placed in a special bag and hidden beneath the floor. Only after cleaning the find in the laboratory were we able to realise how considerable and in what superb condition was the treasure. It consisted of silver shekels and half-shekels, thirty-eight altogether. Closer examination showed that these coins had almost never been in use; many of them indeed had been struck in the year four of the revolt, that is, one year before the last.

Close by, and amidst a thick layer of ashes, another hoard was found several weeks later, consisting of six shekels and six half-shekels in a special bronze box. These coins, too, must have been hidden by the defenders of Masada to prevent their falling into the hands of the Roman conquerors, unlike the bronze coins which were scattered all over the place.

There is a two-fold importance in the discovery of these two hoards of coins – and a third found in one of the chambers of the casemate wall. They constitute the largest group of shekels ever found in one location; and this is the first time that shekels have been discovered in a regular archaeological excavation and in a stratum which belongs without any doubt to the period of the great Jewish revolt. This should put an end once and for all to the controversy of scholars; most of them it is true ascribed such shekels to the period of the revolt, but a few insisted that they belonged to an earlier era. We now know that the majority was right. The shekels in our finds represent all the years of the revolt, from the year one to the very rare year five, the last year the shekel was struck, corresponding to the year 70 AD when the Temple of Jerusalem was destroyed.

Why the coins had been concentrated in this building we shall never know for certain. The name inscribed on the room where the first hoard was found was 'Hillel'. Can it be that this Hillel was the priest who collected part of the coin shipment that was to be sent to the Temple as the regular half-shekel contribution?

Above: The hoard of silver shekels and half-shekels as found. The remains of a cloth bag were still adhering to the coins. *Below:* The shekels after cleaning. Since some of them were struck at the very end of the revolt, this accounts for their superb state of preservation.

9 The Byzantine chapel

To the south of the residential building stands a well-preserved structure which was always the first and most conspicuous ruin to catch the eye of visitors who had been attracted to the Masada summit over the last hundred years. Because of its plan it was easy to identify, and it had in fact long been identified by scholars as a Christian chapel of the Byzantine period, consisting mainly of a long hall and an apse at its eastern end. Its walls are preserved to a considerable height and are covered with plaster bearing such original decoration as pottery sherds and small stones set in geometric patterns and floral designs.

We decided to make an excavation here, too, particularly because of the description by one of the first scholars to visit this site, the well-known de Saulcy, of his finds in this building. De Saulcy, in his *Memoirs*, writes that he saw, scattered about the main hall, portions of mosaic flooring; and he innocently adds that with the help of *baksheesh* which he gave to his Bedouin helpers, he succeeded in clearing parts of the floor. To his deep regret, however, he found that most of it was destroyed, and he was able to take away as a memento only a few pieces, and these he entrusted to the Louvre. When we came to clear this main hall, we found that there was almost no sign either of floor or portions thereof, the result, no doubt, of the not inconsiderable *baksheesh* which de Saulcy had thought fit to hand to his Bedouin companions. Only in the western corner were there a few fragments of coloured mosaic with a geometric design.

We had little hope of finding anything of significance, but since we had started we thought it as well to continue, and we therefore extended our dig to the chambers adjoining the main hall. Running off the north-west corner of the hall was a long room, which apparently served as the living quarters for the church beadles, where we found cupboards and washing vessels. But the principal reward for our intensive work on this site was found in a small chamber off the northern side of the hall. The pile of debris here was very high indeed, and this had apparently discouraged de Saulcy from digging. When we got down to the northern edge of the floor in this room, we glimpsed part of a mosaic which looked as if it might be complete. Unfortunately, the small stones making up the mosaic were not of good quality, and they almost disintegrated at the touch of a hand. Great patience and skill were necessary if the whole floor was to be uncovered

Opposite above: How the main hall of the Byzantine chapel appeared at the beginning of the excavations with the apse in the background – looking east towards the Dead Sea.
Opposite below: A closer view of the unusually decorated wall plaster of the chapel, made of sherds and small stones.

without damage. Happily, one of the English volunteers was an expert who had specialised in dealing with mosaics and she, together with a few other volunteers, spent many days uncovering this mosaic. It was painstaking – and back-breaking – work, bending over the floor and carefully and gently brushing off the earth and dust from every stone. Each day they would manage to uncover another few square inches.

Byzantine mosaic floor of 5th century

The picture on page 114 taken with a wide-angled lens shows the whole of the eastern part of the room, with its walls and windows, as it looked during excavation. When the work of clearance was completed, what lay revealed was a complete Byzantine mosaic floor, one of the most beautiful of those known of this period. Its design is a series of round medallions, in each of which are representations of fruit and plants, such as pomegranates, figs, oranges and grapes. From the style of this mosaic we are able to date the building of the chapel and ascribe it to the 5th century.

Another interesting find was what seems to have been a workshop for the manufacture of stones for mosaics. It contained a quantity of long thin stones, the raw material, no doubt, from which the small mosaic ingredients were cut. A detailed examination of the mosaic floor of the chapel showed that this workshop also belongs to the Byzantine period.

As a result of our excavation, we now know that the Byzantine settlement consisted only of a small group of monks who lived on Masada, just as monks established themselves in other places in the Judean wilderness in the 5th century and later, seeking remote retreats far from the city, but preferably those which had buildings which they could use. The monks on Masada dwelt in small cells scattered over the summit. Some also lived in the caves, as is suggested by the crosses we found painted on the walls. It is assumed that they were forced to leave this location with the Persian or Moslem conquest of the country at the beginning of the 7th century. Since then Masada has remained unoccupied.

Byzantine mosaic workshop containing thousands of thin elongated stones from which mosaic cubes were cut.

The mosaic floor in a room of the chapel seen from above after cleaning and treatment.
The sixteen round medallions contain designs of fruit, an egg-basket
(with cross), flowers and geometric patterns. 5th century A D.

The very gentle work of brushing the earth off the mosaic begins.

Opposite: Two members of the expedition carefully remove earth as the mosaic floor seen in the picture on page 113 began to appear.

Airview of the western palace before excavation, looking east.

10 The western palace

The largest building on Masada is the one standing on the western edge of the rock, close to the Roman ramp. This structure, covering an area of some 36,000 sq. feet, impressed all who visited Masada and prompted earlier scholars to identify it with the palace mentioned by Josephus. We have already shown that the one described by Josephus is at the northern edge. However, the size of the western building, and its plan, justified the estimate that it had the character of a palace. Its general lines could be seen even before we started excavating, but its details and evidence of its functions and purpose became clear only when we had finished.

It may be seen from the plan that the structure comprised three main wings. The south-eastern wing held the dwelling quarters, and consisted of large rooms and small service rooms built round a central court. The second wing, adjoining it to the north, also comprised a series of rooms round a central court, but this was solely a service wing – though it is possible that its northern section may have served as dwelling quarters for

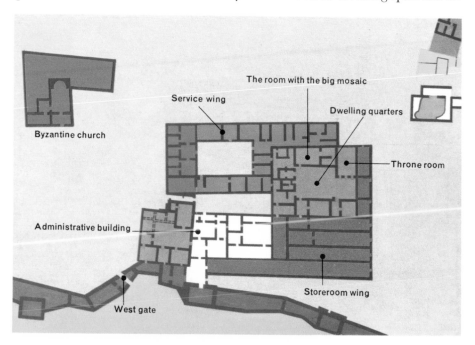

Plan of the western palace. Colours indicate the various
wings: dwelling quarters in mauve; services in orange; storerooms
in red and the administrative building in white.

A corner of the throne room of the palace. Four hollows in the floor probably to hold the canopy of the throne are clearly visible. Note too, the blackended plaster, the result of the big fire which burnt the palace.

the administrative personnel of the palace, for its plan is very similar to that of the 'apartment' building mentioned earlier. The third wing forms the western section of the building and adjoins the two other wings. It originally housed the storerooms and the administrative quarters.

We started excavating the first wing, and its south-eastern corner. This room had three entrances. In its floor were four plastered depressions apparently to hold a canopy or a throne. This area was covered with a formidable layer of ashes, in which we found hundreds of pieces of fine bronze and bone vessels, the kind that would certainly have been used in a palace. The next significant finds were the remains of two columns, plastered and painted. They were found within the court, whose walls, incidentally, bore the white Herodian plaster made to look like stone panels. This area, too, had clearly undergone burning and destruction. The ground to the immediate north was covered with giant heaps of stone and rubble, showing that parts of this structure were originally of two storeys.

Excavation of main Herodian palace
The excavation of this building continued through the two seasons of our expedition, with a group of volunteers averaging fifty to seventy persons working very hard – often requiring the use of cranes – to clear

the stones. But at the end of the dig we found that the very site which had been covered with stone and rubble was nothing more than a large square court with a plastered floor. Today we know that this was the central court of the residential wing, as may be seen in the plan. From this court access was gained to the throne room through the hall at whose entrance stood the two plastered and painted pillars.

Our dig proved that this building was in fact a large and handsome palace from the Herodian period. This palace had not been mentioned by Josephus, who had concentrated, in his description of Masada, on the wondrous palace-villa at the northern point of the great rock. However, there can now be no doubt that this was in fact the ceremonial palace, the palace of the king, *the* palace of Herod at Masada. This is evident not only from its size and plan but also from its ornate construction and the luxury of its appointments. Among the service chambers, for example, we unearthed the kitchen and in it were huge cooking-stoves, the largest found at Masada, each of which could take ten to twelve cooking pots at a time.

At the eastern side of the building, near the rear entrance – which served as the private entrance of the king – we were granted a great reward. In one of the rooms where we had worked for many weeks carefully clearing the debris, we were surprised by a strange and somewhat saddening discovery. About twenty to thirty inches above the level of the original floor we began to turn up fragments of a coloured mosaic strewn in disorder. This was rather astonishing; for on the one hand it revealed a *coloured* floor from the time of Herod – a find which has not yet been duplicated elsewhere on Masada; on the other hand, it showed that at a much later date – after the burning of the building by the Zealots – someone had apparently destroyed the floor during attempts to dig through the piles of debris and rubble presumably in a search for hidden treasure.

But, as I say, the great labour we put into clearing the room did not go unrewarded. When we had finished, we found that the early destruction had damaged only the western half of the floor and left the eastern half untouched. This was in a good state of preservation, and our prize was not only one of the most ancient coloured mosaic floors ever discovered in the country, but undoubtedly also the most beautiful belonging to this period.

Unique coloured mosaic floor uncovered

It is interesting that Herod, even in his buildings at Masada, was reluctant to offend the susceptibilities of his family and Jewish citizens, and he did not therefore resort to representations of the human form and of animals in his mosaics, as was customary in his day. The mosaic we discovered had a geometric design which was very popular in the Hellenistic world of the period, and was in particularly wide use in the island of Delos in the first half of the 1st century B C. But in the centre the theme of mosaic decoration was taken mostly from plant life, and followed designs particularly prominent in Jewish art, such as stylised olive branches, pomegranates, fig leaves, vine leaves, all executed very meticulously by the artists. At the centre of our mosaic floor was a circle containing a number

Overleaf: General view from the north of the room with the coloured mosaic floor. Note the damaged part on the right and the entrance leading from this room to the throne room beyond.

Two pillars, separating the central court from the portico leading to the throne room, being excavated. A layer of ashes and tremendous heaps of stones (top) cover the yet unexcavated central court.

The central court and portico after excavation. Note the well plastered floor.

Large cooking-stove in the palace kitchen.

A moment of great excitement when the first undamaged section of a big multi-coloured mosaic floor begins to appear.

A volunteer cleans part of the border of the mosaic.

Overleaf: The design of the mosaic floor contains motifs popular in Jewish art of the period: pomègranates, vine and fig leaves and a geometrical pattern of circles in the centre.

The damaged floor provides an insight into the technique of the mosaic artists: lines incised on the plaster beneath guide the artist along the borders of the pattern.

of intersecting circles, a common design in Jewish art of this period, frequently found on stone coffins discovered in burial caves, notably in the vicinity of Jerusalem.

The damage done to the western half of the floor, however, did reveal something of interest, for it enabled us to discover the process whereby the mosaic had been laid. Upon the substratum of plaster which the artists had prepared to receive the mosaic stones, lines had been scratched denoting exactly the borders of the floor and the principal patterns, to guide them in the placing of the stones. (A similar method had been used in the laying of the mosaic floors in the upper terrace of the northern palace-villa.) The room with the coloured mosaic, the most ornate room in the western palace, was the entrance hall from which one reached the throne room.

Testimony no less persuasive of the pomp in Herod's western palace was revealed in the north-eastern section of the residential wing. Here we found the private service chambers of the palace, and in the midst of them was a small private bath-house, similar on the whole to the other baths we

Opposite: Private bath in the western palace.

found in Masada and have already mentioned. Here too there was a cold water pool, and here too there was a room with a bath for hot water, but it was, however, heated somewhat differently from the others – not with a hypocaust but from an oven behind the rear wall. The bath itself was plastered, and set against a shallow bow-shaped niche. The floor of this bathroom was a mosaic with a simple design of overlapping squares. The plaster on the walls was well-preserved, and one wall had a small recessed shelf to hold an oil lamp. Incidentally, even the narrow corridor leading to the bathroom was decorated with a mosaic. True, this was less beautiful than the one near the throne room, but to have such a floor at all in a bathroom corridor was impressive. It is of a simple geometric design, a circle within a square consisting of radial segments, executed in coloured mosaic. Some of the colours are unusual.

A small triangular niche in the bathroom to hold an oil lamp.

One of the features that underline again and again the startling contrast between the Masada of Herod and the Masada of the beleaguered Zealots during the revolt came to light here, too, when we discovered on the mosaic the remains of a cupboard, or possibly a stove, which the Zealots had built almost it seems without thought of the luxurious floor on which it rested.

The photograph opposite, shows the beautiful Herodian floor and on it the humble Zealotian installation. We did not remove the installation of the Zealots. We left the remains as we found them, to serve as an illustration of the two main contrasting periods of occupation on the summit of Masada.

As impressive as the first two wings of this palace are the large storerooms in the western wing. They show that the palace was so designed that its occupants could live independently without recourse to the other public buildings and central storehouses on Masada. The dimensions of these

Storeroom wing of the palace after excavation, looking north. On the left the longest storeroom at Masada – 210 feet.
Opposite: The small mosaic floor in the corridor leading to the bathroom. The Zealotian structure in the corner emphasises the contrast between the splendour of Masada in Herod's time and the poverty in the time of the revolt.

Aerial view of the excavated western palace showing all the wings. The swimming-pool and the small palace are bottom right.

palace storerooms are different from those of the large storehouses which we excavated in the north. Indeed, the outside one (in the extreme west) is some 210 feet in length, the longest storeroom we unearthed in Masada.

In Herod's time, these storerooms held more costly and sophisticated items than were stored in Masada's public storehouses. We found evidence of this in the sherds of hundreds of delicate vessels, such as flasks and juglets of cosmetic oil, which were scattered over the floors.

Storerooms found with a great many broken jars

It may be assumed that even in the days of the revolt, when this palace must certainly have been used as administrative offices, its storerooms were used to stock special foods which required special handling. On the floor of the long storeroom we found hundreds, perhaps thousands, of smashed jars amidst a very thick layer of ashes, and it was evident that their contents had been different – and more costly – than the contents of the vessels in the northern storehouses, from the inscriptions in excellent Hebrew which most of them bore. There were such inscriptions as: 'crushed pressed figs'; 'pressed figs'; 'dried figs' – namely, figs pressed into vessels after being pounded or crushed or dried. These cakes of pressed or dried figs would be the most important food item which could be conserved during siege; they were easily stored and preserved, and contained high nutrition value in small bulk.

The main entrance to the palace was from the north, through a long

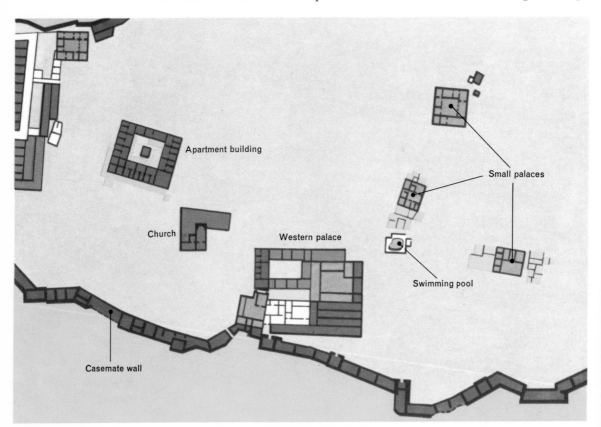

Plan of the central part of Masada showing the distribution of small palaces and the swimming-pool just south-east of the western palace. *Opposite:* The swimming-pool before excavation, looking north-west; the western palace is in the top right. Compare with the picture after excavation on page 135.

corridor whose walls were well plastered. This corridor gave access to the service wing, the storerooms, and the residential wing. In the northern section of the palace, beneath the floor, we discovered a water well, plaster-lined, fed by channels which collected rain water from the roofs. The existence of this well also testifies to the independence of the tenants of this palace from the other buildings on Masada; they were self-sufficient in food and water.

This personal palace of Herod contained all the services he required. We also found a number of smaller and more modest villas, built on the lines of the residential wing of this big palace. Two of these smaller structures are sited to the east of and close to the palace, perched on hillocks which command a magnificent view of the Dead Sea. Two other small structures are close to the storeroom wing: and yet another south of the western palace. There were altogether five of these villas and they were no doubt built for the family of Herod, for his wives and brothers.

Before describing these small palaces, one other structure is worth mentioning. It is located between the western palace and one of the small palaces. Before we started excavating here, we noticed a large depression whose purpose at first eluded us. But after its excavation, which required considerable effort and was exclusively the work of our Danish volunteer mentioned earlier – it became apparent that this, in Herod's time, was

some kind of swimming pool or public bath. It was a massive pool with plastered steps at one end which made bathing possible even with a minimum amount of water. All around it were walls with niches where clothes could be left during bathing. The photograph shows what the pool looked like after its restoration. This swimming pool, like the other water installations built on arid Masada, cannot fail to arouse our respect for the skill, ingenuity and sheer physical labour invested by Herod and his engineers for the conservation and use of water. It is apparent that this pool was in use even in the period of the Jewish revolt. We found coins and other remains of the period on the floor of the pool.

To return to the small villas, they were built, as I have indicated, on the pattern of the large palace, namely, rooms round a large court, one side of which, mostly the southern side, was a roofed hall flanked by two pillars through which one gained access to the principal and most important room of the building. These small palaces were found for the most part in a poorly preserved state. During the revolt they had been occupied by many families who had added walls and partitions so that the palatial character of the building had vanished. But some of these small palaces were ornately decorated. This we discovered from our excavation of one immediately south-east of the storehouse compound, next to a large quarry. The excavation of this building was difficult and offers a typical example of our system of work. The heaps of heavy stone on this site were enormous, completely covering the structure. We had to bring up cranes to remove the stones.

We were specially interested in this building because at the very outset of our dig we noticed in the southern ruins signs of wall paintings identical with the wall paintings in the northern palace-villa and bath-house; and indeed these paintings turned out to be in a good state of preservation.

In the photograph on pages 136 and 7 may be seen one of the walls in this small palace as it appeared immediately after excavation and before it received treatment. It will be noticed that the whole of the bottom part of the wall was decorated with rectangular panels, most of them either black or red. We removed these paintings from the walls, reinforced their backing, cleaned the dust from the paint, and they are today once again on display in their original places in the building, so that the visitor can see for himself the remarkable colours which were used by Herod's artists to decorate these palaces.

The palaces of Masada – the northern, the western, and the five small ones – testify more eloquently than anything else to the judgment of Josephus that Masada was a royal citadel which was intended to give Herod and his family a refuge in time of emergency and to provide living conditions of a standard to which they had become accustomed in Jerusalem and other cities in Palestine.

One other strange building from the Herodian period was found on the southern part of the Masada summit. Before we started digging, we examined the debris on the site. It consisted largely of collapsed walls built

Opposite: Swimming pool after reconstruction; the niches above are for storing clothes.
Overleaf: There is an obvious similarity between this fresco decorating one of the small palace rooms – seen during excavation – and the frescoes of Herod's palace-villa. The Zealots built an oven in the corner of this room with complete disregard for the wall paintings.

of stones in which small niches had been scooped out, rather like the niches in a dovecote. Indeed, because of this likeness, the ruin had been termed by early scholars who visited Masada as the *columbarium*. We set to work, not knowing what we would find, and when the excavation was completed we beheld a circular structure divided into two by a wall with an opening in the centre. The small cells or niches were to be found in all the inner faces of the walls, and in both faces of the dividing wall. There was evidence that this Herodian building had also been used in later periods, both by the Zealots and particularly by the Byzantine monks who had added a floor which was two feet above the level of the original floor. On it we found pottery and other artefacts belonging to the Byzantine period.

So-called 'columbarium' thought to be for remains of cremations

On the face of it, the numerous small cells, if not the structural plan of the building, are reminiscent of many niched walls found in caves in the country, mostly in the south but also in the north. Various theories have been put forward by scholars to explain their function. Some held them to have been dovecotes (or pigeon-coops), for the raising of pigeons for the

The circular *columbarium* after excavation, looking west. The niches on the inner face of the circular wall and on both sides of the dividing wall led to the theory that they were used as dovecotes.

collection of pigeon droppings for agricultural fertiliser. Others suggested that they were dovecotes associated with some form of worship. However, the smallness of the niches, on the one hand, and the lavishness of the building, on the other, provoked doubts. To settle the problem, we decided on a practical test. Moshe Yoffe, our construction expert, happens to raise pigeons at home, and one day he brought to Masada a very small pigeon for the test. The picture on the right shows him trying to get the pigeon into a niche, first by cajolery, then by force, but to no avail. The niches were too small.

It is our conviction that this building, like similar though larger buildings discovered in Italy, was designed to receive the remains of cremations. It is probable that Herod built it for the burial of his servants, ministers or other members of his court who were not Jewish.

Two buildings, square not circular, but with similar niches in their walls, were found in the north-western part of the wall; it is possible that they fulfilled the same function.

The expedition's chief mason trying unsuccessfully to get a small pigeon into one of the niches.

A closer view of the niches in the *columbarium*, looking east.

Various pieces of cloth as they were found on the floor of the
casemate in the wall; they consist of parts of bags and tunics.

11 The casemate wall

Except for the northern tip of the rock of Masada, the entire summit is enclosed by a wall. At the northern end, the wall reaches only to the southern section of the palace-villa, so that this villa is outside the wall – a fact which fits the description of Josephus.

Even before we started excavating, we knew from Josephus, from air photographs and from a preliminary examination of the ground, that this was a casemate wall, that is, a double wall with the space between divided into chambers by partitioning walls. The casemate type was very popular in the 1st century BC. The chambers within the wall had both a utilitarian and a military purpose, being used as storerooms or dwelling-rooms for the troops, and serving as a base for the building of battlements and firing embrasures. This type of construction was also most economical in building materials. This is how Josephus describes the wall:

He [Herod] also built a wall round about the entire top of the hill, seven furlongs long; it was composed of white stone; its height was twelve and its breadth eight cubits; there was also erected upon that wall thirty-eight towers, each of them fifty cubits high; out of which you might pass into lesser edifices which were built on the inside round the entire wall.

The measurements of the wall, as we found from our excavations, on the whole matched those given by Josephus. It is some 1,400 yards in length and about four-and-a-half yards in width (that is, the space between the two walls of the casemate, and not including their thickness). The measurements of height given by Josephus are no doubt exaggerated. This was due probably to an optical illusion for anyone looking at it from the outside: the height of the wall was not uniform: it varied with the variations in the terrain. Where the rock itself is high, the wall upon it looks higher than it is; and vice versa.

Another detail on which Josephus is inaccurate concerns the material with which the wall was built. We found that it consisted wholly of the hard dolomite stone which was quarried on Masada. Josephus' report that it was 'composed of white stone' was prompted however by the impression received by the observer from the outside, for the wall was covered with a white plaster, fragments of which we found in many places.

There were about 110 rooms inside the wall and towers, and they varied

Inaccuracies of Josephus' description of casemate wall

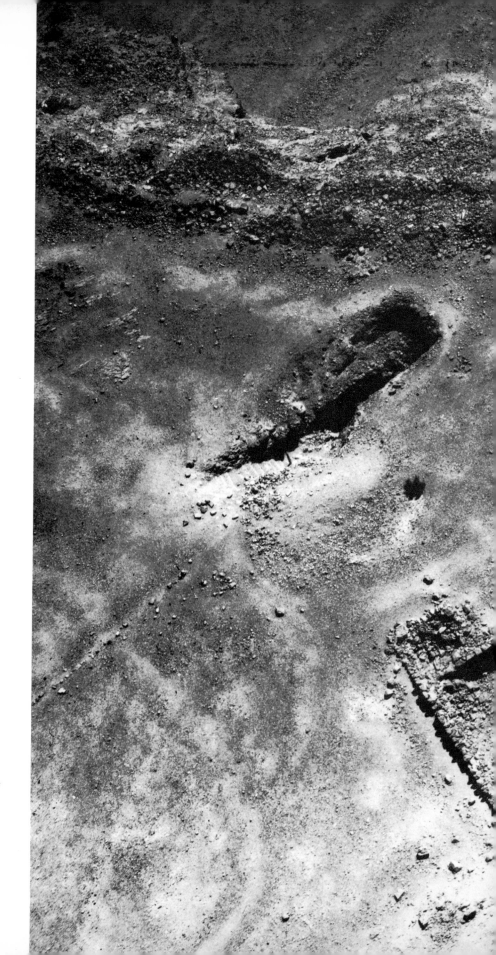

The casemate wall is clearly visible in this vertical airview of south-east Masada before excavation. Above is the entrance to the underground water reservoir cut in the rock.

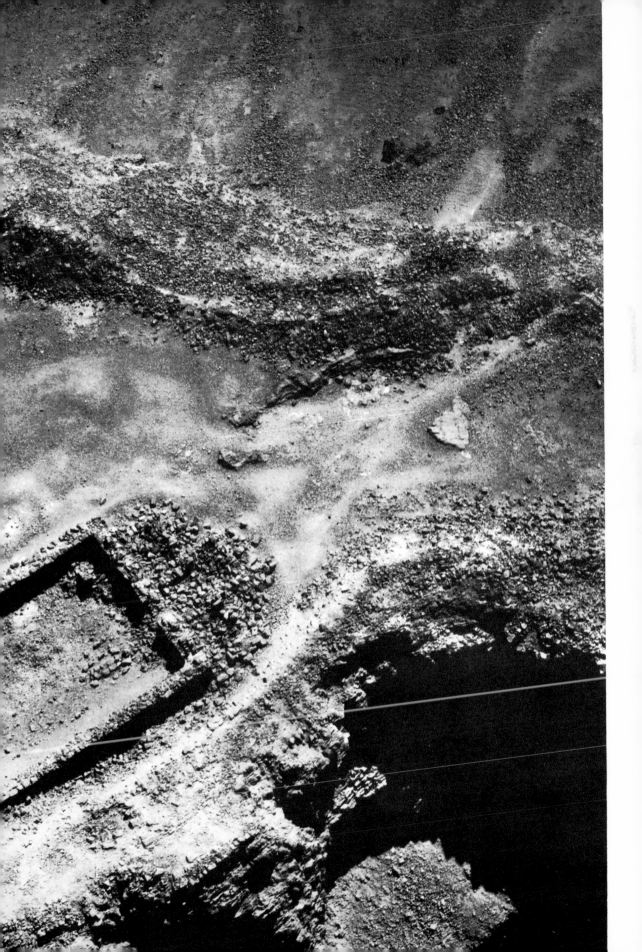

This plaited palm-frond basket, found in one of the casemates, was most
probably made from palms grown in the nearby oasis of Ein-Gedi.

in size, ranging in length from six yards to thirty-eight yards, with the
medium sized chambers averaging thirteen to sixteen yards. For the most
part the face of the natural rock had not been smoothed, and the original
floors of the chambers were rough and pitted.

Our aim in excavating the wall had largely been to clarify the method of
its construction, its measurements and its character. But in the event, the
dig here proved more rewarding than at any other location, yielding the
most impressive discoveries on the period of the revolt. As might have been
expected, the casemate rooms offered an excellent solution to the problem
of housing for the numerous rebels and their families, for the Masada of
Herod had not been designed for such a purpose nor for the occupation of
so many. The storehouses could not be used as dwellings, for the Jewish
defenders needed them also for stores. As for the palaces, they could house
only a few families; and several of the public buildings were used by the
Zealots for administrative and military command purposes. There was

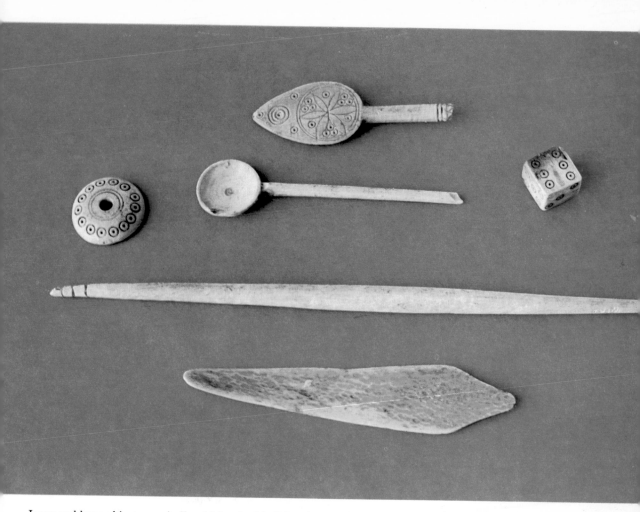

Ivory and bone objects: a spindle-whirl and stick (*left and centre*);
egg-spoons (*top*); dice (*right*); and spatula (*bottom*).

thus no place left on Masada able to meet a large-scale housing need, and
so the rooms in the casemate wall were a godsend to them.

The Zealots had made architectural additions to these casemate chambers – almost the only site on Masada where they had done so – and pretty
modest additions they were, too. They had built partitions in the large
chambers, dividing them into smaller dwelling units which could serve a
few families, and they had added cupboards to the wall and built mud
ovens. As we excavated these casemate rooms, we found ourselves re-
capturing the daily lives of the Zealots, and we stood awed by the evidence
of what had taken place in the final moments before their suicide.

Excavation here was very difficult. Along the entire length of 1,400 yards,
the walls had collapsed, some outwards, over the precipice, some inwards,
so that the whole wall with its casemate chambers looked like a huge chain
of stones winding round Masada. Scores of volunteers – almost half our
manpower – worked for eleven months on the task of clearing the ruins of

*Casemate rooms had
been used as
dwelling units by
Zealots*

the wall. As an indication of what it looked like before the dig, the picture above shows part of the southern section. It is typical; and it is almost impossible to make out the double walls. But after excavation, the two walls are well defined, as is seen in the later photograph of the same section.

In contrast to the public buildings, which we found had all been completely destroyed, right down to their foundations, as recorded by Josephus, the dwelling rooms of the Zealots within the casemate wall had for the most part not been fired. It seemed as if the defenders of Masada had said to themselves in their last moments that it would not matter much if such humble dwelling chambers fell into the hands of the conquerors. And so we found many of their domestic vessels strewn about the floors. Because of Masada's great aridity, even vessels made of delicate materials were found in a good state of preservation. They included cosmetic items, a wooden comb, a box for eye-paint, and numerous vessels of stone – of the type known as 'measuring vessels' – which were in daily use particularly because

Opposite: A section of the southern casemate wall before excavation, looking east. In the distance on the right, some 1,000 feet below the top of Masada, are the Roman siege camps.

Above: The same casemate after excavation, showing two parallel walls and the mud-plastered floor. The Roman camps are again visible below and on the right the Dead Sea and mountains of Moab.

Bronze pan and jug found hidden under the floors of the casemate wall.

Clay oil-lamps typical of the 1st century AD. Scores of these were found in various rooms belonging to the Zealots.

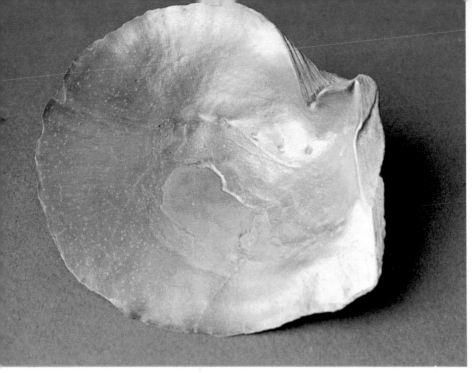

A cosmetic palette made of a shell from the Red Sea.

Some cosmetic equipment found in the Zealots' dwellings. *Left to right*: twin palette;
two bronze eye shadow sticks; clay perfume phials; bronze mirror case; and a wooden
comb.

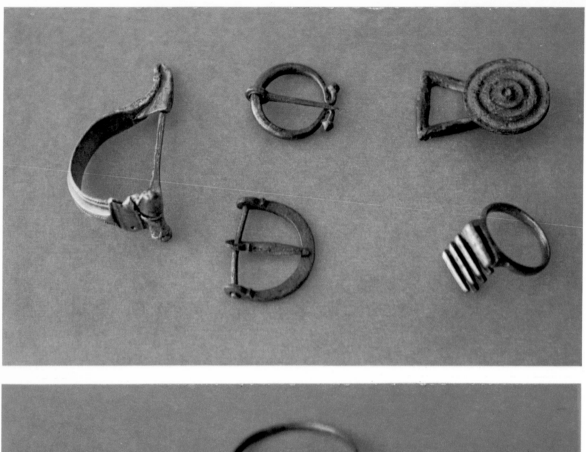

Top: Various bronze objects: fibula (*left*); two buckles (*centre*); ring key (*bottom right*); and knob (*top right*).

Bottom: Signet rings; in the bottom row the two on the left are of gold.

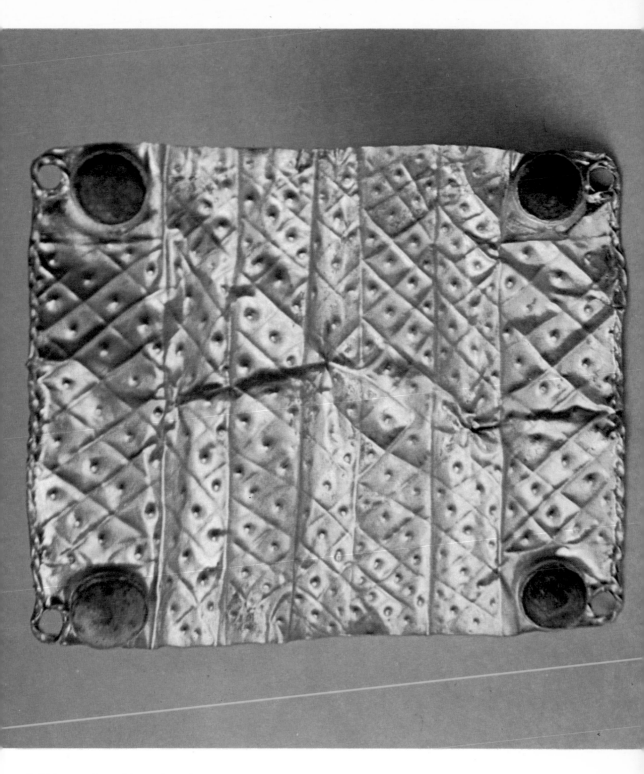

Gold breast-plate with semi-precious stones.

Vessels made of soft stone including measuring mugs and bowl; marks
from the carving instrument and the lathe are visible.

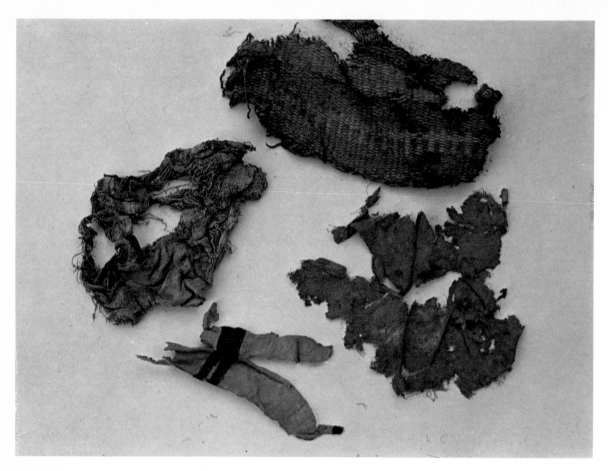

Some exquisitely woven fragments of wool fabric.

stone was proof against ritual impurity. We also found remains of cloth and sacking on the floors and these represent today the earliest and most complete collection of textile material from the Roman period discovered so far. Before the dig at Masada, that distinction went to the cloth which we had discovered in the caves of Bar Kochba dating from 132–5 A D.

Often, as we would clear a casemate chamber, we had the feeling that it had only just been abandoned; for there was a familiar domestic atmosphere, with the white wall above the cooking stoves smudged with soot. There were rooms we excavated which at first glance had not been burnt, but we would find in a corner a heap of spent embers containing the remains of clothing, sandals, domestic utensils and cosmetic items, which told the poignant story of how, perhaps only minutes before the end, each family had collected together its humble belongings and set them on fire. This also is how Josephus describes what happened. These small heaps of embers were perhaps the sights that moved us most during our excavation.

The dwellings in the casemate rooms did not suffice for all, and close to the wall and the public buildings, and even on the open ground of the summit, we found the remains of modest structures made of mud, or just

This heap of embers in the corner of the casemate is grim evidence
of the last tragic moments of the defenders of Masada.

*Remains of huts
containing evidence
of the final moments*huts with thin walls, which had been put up hurriedly without doubt to
house the additional families who had gathered in Masada at the end of
the revolt. In these huts, too, we discovered signs of what had taken place
in the final moments; they were most evident in the kitchens, near the
cooking stoves, where it seemed as if life had been cut off suddenly. And
here, too, we unearthed an interesting collection of various types of stoves
and fire-places, the most common being stoves with two hollows. In one place
we found cooking pots and kettles, almost complete, strewn on the floor
next to the stove; and in the corner of one room there was a cooking pot
completely charred. A young man from a *kibbutz* uncovered one such pot
in a primitive hut. There were also stoves of a superior type with recesses
shaped in the upper part probably to hold bowls while food was being
poured into them; and we found particularly large stoves as well, like these;
near the stoves were found remains of oil or flour jars, and faggots which had
been left unused.

In the chambers of the casemate wall we discovered hundreds of coins
from the period of the Jewish revolt, some of them in groups of two to three
hundred. Most of them were scattered about the floors as if they had been
flung away as worthless objects (for of what value were they when the end
was so near?). In a few places we found hoards hidden under the floor.

Excavation of the casemate rooms also enabled us better to understand
the military problem which faced the Masada defenders. At several of the
key strategic points along the wall, such as those dominating the 'snake
path' in the east (but also at sites overlooking the southern slope, which is
particularly steep), we found on the floors of the rooms more than a dozen
huge, round stones, each weighing about 100 lbs. It is possible that these
stones which were kept on the roofs fell through on to the floors when the
roofs caved in. Rolled down the slopes, they would certainly have proved
lethal to anyone trying to clamber up and reach the summit by the customary routes; yet it was clear that such weapons had never been used. The
reason for this is that the Romans chose to assault Masada at one point alone,
on the western side. To this end, they laid a huge ramp and at the head of it
they erected siege towers and catapults. From these they directed their catapult 'fire' at a narrow sector – to effect a breach which they would then storm.
Covering fire was provided by archers. And, indeed, all round this sector
we found hundreds of ballistic stones the size of grapefruit which had been
hurled at Masada by the Roman catapults. The desperate military plight
of the Masada defenders is well illustrated by a comparison of this heap
of Roman missiles with the 'rolling' stones which had been left unneeded
and unused (see pictures on pages 162–3).

The discovery of hundreds of these catapult stones gives tangibility to
Josephus' description of the Roman assault on Masada, under the command
of General Silva.

From an historical view-point, however, the most significant of our
discoveries in the rooms of the casemate wall were undoubtedly the scrolls.
We shall deal with them later.

Stove, jar and unused faggots exactly as discovered.

Overleaf: A typical Zealot dwelling within the casemate wall; there is soot on the wall behind the mud cooking-stove, a niche which was used as a cupboard and a small hollow (*left*) for an oil lamp.

Recesses to hold bowls are plainly visible in this stove.

The daily life of the Zealots is preserved by this stove with cooking utensils still lying nearby – the pots even have soot on them still.

A young *kibbutz* member patiently unearths a cooking pot in the corner of a room.

Another cooking pot is recovered from the debris.

Below: A group of stones each weighing about 100 lbs. in the casemate wall, close to a strategic point above the 'snake path'.

Left: This heap of Roman missiles, each about the size of a large orange, was found near the residence of the Zealots, close to the spot in the wall where the Roman breach was made.

163

12 The ritual bath (*mikve*)

We were much surprised by what came to light as we uncovered one of the chambers in the southern section of the casemate wall. When we had cleared all the debris from this room, what we saw was a system of three adjacent pools – one large, one medium-sized and one small. Steps had been built in the two larger pools so that one could reach the bottom, and in the wall between them there was a connecting hole through which water could flow from one to the other. Moreover, as may be seen in the picture, there was an open, plastered, water conduit leading into the first – the largest – pool, and this conduit no doubt served to collect and channel rainwater from the roof of the room and its surroundings.

Important discovery of the ritual immersion bath

This find immediately suggested to us that what we had discovered was a ritual immersion bath – *Mikve* in Hebrew – and this we announced at our routine press conference. The news that we had brought to light a *mikve* from the period of the Second Temple quickly spread throughout the country, arousing particular interest in orthodox religious quarters and

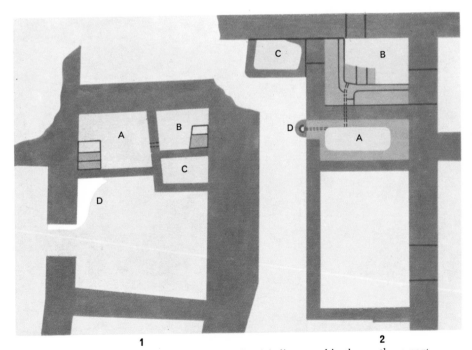

Plan of the southern *mikve* (1) and the other *mikve* (2) discovered in the northern part of Masada in the court of the administration building. They are identical in their functional elements: A, pool for collecting rain-water through conduit or cesspit, D; B, the actual bath connected to A by a pipe; C, the smallest pool for washing of hands and feet before immersion in the *mikve* B.

The ritual bath or *mikve* in the southern wall after excavation. Note the three pools and the plastered water conduit on the left.

Talmudic scholars; for the traditional Jewish laws of the Talmud relating to the ritual bath are quite complex, and no *mikve* has so far been discovered belonging to this very period, the period when much of the relevant traditional law governing the *mikve* was written and enacted.

This special interest in the *mikve* led to one of my strangest meetings on the Masada summit, and it indicates, too, how wide was Masada's appeal to our people, and how it spoke to each in his own language. We received information one day, during the excavations, that Rabbi David Muntzberg, specialist in the laws of the *mikve,* and Rabbi Eliezer Alter, were anxious to visit Masada and see for themselves the *mikve* we had discovered. I signalled that I would be pleased to receive them, and one hot day, during the hottest hour of the afternoon, the two Rabbis arrived on the summit. They had climbed the tough 'snake path' on the east face under the broiling sun, wearing their characteristic heavy garments, and accompanied by a group of their Hassidic followers. Though they are no longer young, neither agreed to rest when they finally reached the top; nor did they wish to see any of the handsome structures of King Herod. They wanted one thing only: to be led directly to the *mikve*. We took them there, and the aged Rabbi Muntzberg immediately went into one of the pools, a tape-measure in his hand, to examine whether in fact the volume of this *mikve* was the 'forty measures' required by the ritual law. I photographed him and his companions in the process. It remains one of my favourite pictures of the Masada dig. Spiritually, these people had been deeply stirred by what apparently was a very humble structure, though, admittedly, dramatically sited within a wall at the edge of a steep escarpment. This *mikve* meant more to them than anything else on Masada.

I confess that during Rabbi Muntzberg's examination I was rather anxious. What would be his finding? His face throughout bore a serious expression, and at times he furrowed his brows as if in doubt as to whether the bath was *kosher*. But when he completed his meticulous study, he announced with beaming face and to the delight of us all, that this *mikve* was indeed a ritual bath 'among the finest of the finest, seven times seven'.

How had this *mikve* been built? According to Jewish religious law, such a bath, without which no orthodox Jew could live, particularly in those days, had to be filled for the most part with rain-water flowing into it directly, and not brought to it with buckets or the like. This of course was not possible in Palestine during most months of the year, when there is simply no rain, and the law therefore prescribes that it is sufficient if part of the water is 'pure'; additional water, drawn and brought from elsewhere and not direct-flowing rain-water, becomes 'purified' on contact with the pure water. They therefore built two pools. In one – in ours at Masada the one nearest the entrance – water was gathered during the rainy season and stored; the second was the actual bath itself. Before using it, they would open the bung in the connecting pipe allowing some drops of the stored, direct, rain-water to flow into the bathing pool and thus purify it.

The third pool in the Masada *mikve*, the smallest, which was not con-

A moment of great excitement when the Rabbis – experts in the rules governing ritual baths – examine the *mikve*.

nected to the other two pools, was for actual cleansing purposes (as distinct from ritual purification), for washing the hands and feet before immersion in the *mikve*.

That this was not the only *mikve* on Masada, and that it had clearly been constructed according to standard ritual regulations, we found out just before the end of our excavation season when we unearthed an almost identical *mikve* on the other side of the summit, in the north-eastern corner of the large administration building to the west of the storehouses. This building, as we have seen, had also been in use both during the period of the Zealots and later at the time of the Roman garrison. We discovered the *mikve* when we excavated its courtyard. Here, too, may be seen the carefully installed communicating pipe between the 'pure' water pool and the immersion pool. This device, incidentally, shed interesting light on a number of hitherto obscure passages in the Mishna. It also illustrates, as do the inscriptions about tithes mentioned earlier, that the defenders of Masada were devout Jews, so that even here, on dry Masada, they had gone to the arduous lengths of building these ritual baths in scrupulous conformity with the injunctions of traditional Jewish law.

Bath built strictly in accordance with Jewish law

13 The scrolls

Before starting the excavations at Masada, we dreamed of the possibility of finding scrolls there. I say 'dreamed' because the hope that we would could not be very bright. Hitherto, all the scrolls which had been found in the vicinity of the Dead Sea had been discovered only in caves, where they had been hidden intentionally, and where the only damage they suffered – comparatively slight – had been damage by nature, such as mild dampness, or by the nibbling of small animals. Now, as we approached Masada, we asked ourselves: 'Had the Zealots hidden their writings before committing suicide? And if they had, would any of them still be preserved? And would we find them?'

Exciting discovery of scroll in casemate room
As I say, these were simply reflections on our part, hopeful speculation; and so our great excitement may be imagined when, only a few weeks after we started digging, we found our first scroll. It was discovered in one of the rooms in the casemate wall (room 1,039, as it is referred to in our field charts). After clearing more than six foot of debris, we had got down close to the floor. The room had not been burned, and it contained a large collection of vessels, cloth, mats, baskets, and leather articles. We thought perhaps that the Roman garrison had assembled here a mixed bag of articles gathered in the vicinity. Then came the first serious find, important not only in itself but also in relation to the other finds. Strewn over a small area of the floor in the southern corner of the room were seventeen silver shekels. They were in excellent condition. The inscriptions in Hebrew *Shekel Israel* and *Jerusalem the Holy* were completely clear. So were the Hebrew letters *shin alef, shin beth, shin gimel, shin daleth* and *shin he. Shin* is the first letter of *shana*, the Hebrew word for 'year', and the other letters represent the numbers 1,2,3,4,5 respectively. The markings on the coins were thus 'year one', 'year two', 'year three', 'year four' and 'year five' – each denoting in which year of the revolt (which lasted five years) the coin had been struck. Until this discovery, the total number of shekels struck in the rare 'year five' known to exist in the world was only six; here, among the seventeen shekels we found, three were of 'year five'. Here, too, as with the two large hoards we found later and which we have already mentioned, silver shekels were found for the first time in a systematic archaeological excavation, and in an archaeological stratum clearly belonging to the period of the revolt.

Opposite: A tense moment while detaching fragments of papyrus from basket remains in the room of the scrolls.

Shmaryahu Guttman using a puffer to clean the silver shekels still lying on the floor as they were found.

A portion of the Book of Psalms scroll as it was found; enough could just be seen with the naked eye to identify it.

Both sides of four of the shekels: (1) year two; (2) year three; (3) year four; (4) the rare year five, i.e. the year Jerusalem and the Temple were destroyed by the Romans.

About three feet away from the shekels the first scroll was found. All the details of this discovery are sharp in my mind. In the early hours of the afternoon, while I was in one of the northern storerooms, Shmaryahu Guttman came running to me, followed by some of the volunteers working with him, and flourished before me a piece of parchment. It was so black and creased that only with difficulty could one make anything out. But a quick examination on the spot showed us immediately that here was a fragment from the *Book of Psalms*, and we could even identify the chapters: the section ran from Psalm 81 to Psalm 85. A little while later we also found another part of the scroll, which completed the top part of the first fragment. After this scroll fragment had been treated by the elderly technical expert, Professor Bieberkraut, and photographed by his wife Helena with infra-red film, this writing on parchment could be read with ease.

This discovery is of extraordinary importance for scroll research. It is

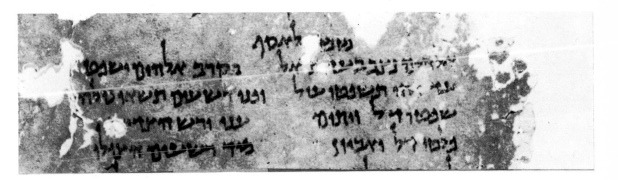

The beginning of Psalm 82 is clearly visible in this infra-red photo. The text of this scroll is identical with the traditional Hebrew version, both in wording and the division of the Psalms.

not only that this is the first time that a parchment scroll has been found not in a cave, and in circumstances where it was possible to date it without the slightest doubt. It could not possibly be later than the year 73 AD, the year Masada fell. As a matter of fact, this scroll was written much before – perhaps twenty or thirty years earlier; and it is interesting that this section from the *Book of Psalms*, like the other biblical scrolls which we found later, is almost exactly identical (except for a few very minor changes here and there) to the text of the biblical books which we use today. Even the division into chapters and psalms is identical with the traditional division. This not only testifies to the strength and faithfulness of the Jewish tradition, but it enables us to learn many things about the development of the biblical text, particularly in the light of the fact that many of the scrolls of biblical books which were discovered in Qumran and in the caves north of Masada, contained significant textual changes from the accepted traditional text. On the second section of the fragment that we found lay several bronze coins struck in the second and third years of the revolt. We could not have hoped to find more effective testimony to the date of our scroll. In the same room in the casemate's wall we found another few fragments of scrolls, among them one from the *Book of Leviticus*.

But the scroll which gave us the greatest surprise was discovered in the south-eastern corner of the room. This was not a large fragment, and it appeared, as with other fragments, that it had been cut and torn intentionally. Had this been the work of the Roman garrison? It is possible. Josephus writes that one of the ways in which the Roman soldiers persecuted the Jews was tearing books of the Bible before their eyes. Apparently, the Roman soldiers occupied this room for some time, as is evidenced by a

172

number of Latin papyri, some kind of military documents, which may be ascribed to the Roman garrison. The torn scroll fragment, when photographed, was found to contain Hebrew writing. When I began reading it, I came across a line which read, 'The song of the sixth Sabbath sacrifice on the ninth of the second month'. Seeing this and a few other lines, I was suddenly struck by the amazing fact that this text was exactly the same as the text of one of the scrolls discovered in Qumran, in cave four. That scroll was a very definite sectarian scroll which details 'songs of the Sabbath sacrifices' dealing with each Sabbath and its date.

The sixth Sabbath could have fallen on the ninth of the second month only on the basis of the special calendar used by the Qumran sect. This calendar divided the year into 364 days – twelve months of thirty days each, and one additional day at the end of every three months. The first day of the first month, namely, the month of *Nissan*, always fell on a Wednesday, the day of the creation of the luminaries, which determined the division of time.

The big question was: 'What has this sectarian scroll to do with Masada?' Most scholars believe that the sect which had the scrolls of Qumran was the Essenes, described at length by Philo the Alexandrian and by Josephus, and also mentioned in the writings of Pliny, who was with the conquering Roman army. These say that the Essenes lived on the western shore of the Dead Sea in an area which very much suggests the location of Khirbet Qumran. A minority of scholars have long suggested that the Qumran sect should be identified with the Sicarii Zealots, the very Zealots who occupied Masada. For these scholars, of course, the discovery of this sectarian scroll in Masada was, on the face of it, important support for the truth of their theory. However, I believe that the evidence in the hands of the majority of scholars who identify the Qumran sect with the Essenes is so strong that one needs to find another explanation for the presence of a Qumranic scroll in the Masada stronghold of the Zealots. It seems to me that the discovery of this scroll serves as proof indeed that the Essenes also participated in the great revolt against the Romans. For some reason a distorted picture has emerged about these Essenes, and this is mostly the fault of Philo's descriptions. There were scholars who sought to imply from these descriptions that the Essenes were pacifists, in the modern meaning of the term; but this was not so. They refrained from participating in wars so long as these wars were not in accordance with their concept, namely, wars pre-ordained by God. But if they had reached the recognition that the great revolt was in fact the ordained war against the Romans, there would have been no reason, in terms of their own beliefs and concepts, not to take part in it. Moreover, there is in fact direct evidence in the writings of Josephus of Essene participation in the war.

It will be recalled that Josephus, at the beginning of the revolt, was one of the Jewish commanders, responsible for the Galilee region, and he certainly was acquainted with other commanders of the revolt. When he lists the names of the commanders of the revolt and their sectors, he relates that the commander of the important central sector – which included Lod, Jaffa, Jamnia etc – was someone named John the Essene. Is it likely that only one Essene joined the revolt and became an outstanding commander?

I think not. It is more likely that a considerable number of Essenes also joined the rebellion. And after the country had been destroyed and Masada remained the sole stronghold and outpost in the war against the Romans, it is likely that all who had fought together and survived found shelter there, among them also the Essene participants. It would have been natural for all such groups to have brought with them their holy writings. This, it seems to me, explains the presence of the Qumranic sectarian scroll in Masada. At all events, this small scroll fragment found in casemate 1,039 will assuredly remain more than any other discovery of ours in Masada as a subject of research and stormy debate among scholars of ancient scrolls and of the history of the Second Temple period.

This was not the only casemate in which scrolls were found. We discovered other fragments, for example, in one of the chambers in the eastern sector, just north of the 'snake path'. The excavation work in this sector was very difficult because large sections of the outside wall had collapsed and they needed to be strengthened and supported before we could start digging.

What we discovered was a piece of white leather which contained the last chapter of the *Book of Psalms*, namely, Psalm 150, 'Praise ye the Lord ... Praise Him with the sound of the trumpet.' The writing on it was so faded and the colour of the parchment so light that it almost escaped our notice, and indeed when it was being cleaned one of the volunteers thought that what she was holding in her hand was a piece of newspaper.

To the south of the 'snake path', in casemate 1,109, we found another scroll, perhaps one of the most important for the study of Jewish and Hebrew literature of the Second Temple period. In the northern part of the room, near the floor, we came upon a few crushed and creased scroll fragments, as may be seen in the picture on the next page.

When they were opened and photographed by the infra-red process, we were able to read them as if they had been written the same day, and our delight may be imagined when it became clear that these were fragments of the lost original Hebrew text of the scroll *The Wisdom of Ben-Sira*. Ben-Sira lived in the first half of the 2nd century BC, several decades before the Hasmonean period. His book, which was widely known in his day, just missed being included in the Old Testament canon, and it is widely quoted in the *Talmud*, the ancient Rabbis (The Sages) referring to it and quoting its proverbs in the same authoritative way as they quote from the books of the Bible. However, since it was not included in the canonical works of the Old Testament, its original Hebrew text disappeared in the course of time, and it was preserved for us only in translation, the most notable being the Greek. This was the work of Ben-Sira's grandson, towards the end of the 2nd century BC. This Greek translation was included by the Church in the books of the Apocrypha, and is known as *Ecclesiasticus*. Modern scholars had long felt that there were corruptions in the Greek copies and some even held that the grandson's translation had not always been faithful to the Hebrew text.

Part of scroll found is lost Hebrew original of Ecclesiasticus

A dramatic turning point in the *Ben-Sira* research came in 1896 with the discovery of portions of a Hebrew text of *Ben-Sira* among the mediaeval manuscripts found in the *Cairo Geniza* – the *geniza* (hidden sacred writings) of the old Cairo synagogue. This discovery immediately set off a fierce controversy among scholars. The majority believed that this was indeed a copy of the original Hebrew text of *Ben-Sira*, even though there were a number of copyist's corruptions, since this copy had been made in the Middle Ages. A minority of scholars, however, argued that this was a translation back to Hebrew made in the Middle Ages, from the Greek or the Syriac translations of the original Hebrew.

Well, here at Masada we had just discovered parts of the original Hebrew text of *The Wisdom of Ben-Sira*, and the writing of our scroll could be dated to the first half of the 1st century BC. We could now compare this with the text of the *Cairo Geniza*. The comparison put an end to the controversy, for it showed quite clearly that the two texts are basically identical, namely, that the text in the *Cairo Geniza* on the whole represents the original *Ben-Sira* Hebrew text. I say 'on the whole' because there are, of course, some corruptions, some earlier, some later, some the fault of copyists, some the fault of editors. But the model was clearly the original *Ben-Sira*.

Our discovery may have stopped the controversy over, but not the study of, *Ben-Sira*. Indeed it has opened a new chapter in research on this book, which is one of the most important apocryphal works and one of the greatest

A portion of the *Ecclesiasticus* scroll as found. A seam can be
seen between two sheets of the scroll.

An infra-red photograph of part of the scroll of *Ecclesiasticus* reveals
it to be the lost Hebrew original of this book; this copy can be dated
to the first half of the first century B.C.

Hebrew books of the period of the Second Temple. Here, for example, is a translation of one of the pages found in Masada:

Let me now hymn the praises of men of piety
    Our fathers in their generations
Great honour did the Most High allot
    And His greatness from the days of old
Men who wielded dominion over the earth in their royalty
    And men of renown in their might
And counsellors in their discernment
    And all-seeing in their prophecy
Princes of the nation in their statesmanship
    And leaders in their decrees
Clever of speech in their scribal instruction
    And speakers of wise sayings at their festivities
Devisers of psalms according to rule
    And authors of proverbs in books
Men of resource and supported with strength
    And living at ease in their dwelling-places
All these were honoured in their generation
    And in their days had glory
Some of them there are who have left a name
    That men might tell of it in their inheritance
And some of them there are who have no memorial
    So that there was an end of them when they came to their end
They were as though they had not been
    And their children after them
Nevertheless these were men of piety
    And their goodness shall not be cut off
With their seed their goodness remaineth sure
    And their inheritance to their children's children
In their covenant their seed abideth
    And their children's children for their sakes
And for ever their seed abideth
    And their glory shall not be erased
And their body is buried in peace
    But their name liveth unto all generations
The assembly recounteth their wisdom
    And their praise the congregation relateth
Noah the righteous was found blameless
    In the season of destruction he became the continuator
For his sake there was a remnant
    And by reason of the covenant with him the flood ceased.

Having mentioned this apocryphal book, we should also mention the discovery of another scroll which was found in one of the wall towers to the west of the western palace. This tower rises to a great height and at the top of it there were remains of a monk's cell from the Byzantine period. After we had removed the foundations and had cleared a layer of almost nine feet of debris, we got near to the floor of the structure. It was apparent that here too, during the period of its occupation by the Roman garrison, all sorts of articles in the area had been gathered and thrown as if it were a garbage heap, and among such articles we found beautiful Nabatean vessels which enabled us to determine their exact date.

Because of the dryness of the atmosphere and the discovery here of mats, baskets, pieces of wood and so on, we had the feeling that this was a site where we might find a scroll. There was almost a 'scroll smell' about the place, and indeed when we got right down to the floor of the room, we found a scroll fragment. The credit for this find went to a doctor from London. The fragment we found is small but its importance is great. It is written in Hebrew and it contains portions of the original Hebrew text of one of the pseudo-epigraphical works which has also disappeared with time, namely, the *Book of Jubilees*. This book, which describes the journeys of the patriarchs in the *Book of Genesis* in accordance with the special calendar of the Qumran sect, had, as I say, disappeared in its original text and has been preserved largely in its various translations into Greek, Ethiopian and Latin.

Book of Jubilees

The one scroll which was found outside the bounds of the casemate chambers and the dwellings of the Zealots was discovered in a place we could never have thought of. At the end of the first season of excavation, after seven months of work, a small heap of debris was still left from the huge mound which had covered the wall of the upper terrace of the northern palace-villa. This small heap which we had not managed to excavate was at its western edge, and all we could do was to mark it and postpone its clearance until the second season. On the very first day of the second season, early in the afternoon, it fell to a young lad from a *kibbutz* in Western Galilee to discover in the western corner of the court in front of the large wall, fragments of a scroll scattered among the ruins. This discovery provoked great excitement and was taken as a happy omen for our future work. Parts of the fragments had been eaten away, but those that were undamaged were very well preserved and we could immediately identify them as several chapters from the *Book of Leviticus*, chapters eight to twelve, and to note that this scroll too was absolutely identical with the traditional text of *Leviticus*. Moreover, there was the same division into sections, the traditional division into 'open' and 'closed' ones, that is, sections which begin after an empty line-space at the end of the previous one, and those which begin after a small space in the same line.

Another fragment of Book of Leviticus found

How this scroll reached this location we shall never know. Maybe it was blown here by the wind during the destruction of Masada and was buried among the ruined debris; or perhaps it was thrown here by one of the Roman soldiers. At all events, its discovery here might be called an archaeological 'miracle'.

The discovery of the next two scrolls also surprised us by their location, and shed much light on an understanding of the building in which they were found, as we shall now see.

The synagogue after excavation; benches and two rows of columns remain.
It is oriented towards Jerusalem, in the distance. Below Masada, Silva's
camp is visible on the right and the expedition camp on the left.

14 The synagogue and its scrolls

At the very beginning of our first season of excavations, while digging in the north-western section of the wall of Masada, we came upon a strange structure adjoining the wall, so close that it seemed part of the wall, even though it projected substantially inwards and eastwards, inside Masada. It was unlike any of the buildings we had excavated up to then in the case-mate wall. Early in the dig we noticed what looked like benches plastered with clay protruding from the debris inside the building, next to the walls. Gradually, pillars began to appear, made in sections, and when we had finished excavating, what appeared before us was a rectangular structure with benches all round the walls, tier upon tier, all plastered with clay. On the eastern side there was an opening. In the centre were two rows of columns, three columns in the southern row and two in the northern. The north-western corner of the building was a kind of cell which merged into the casemate wall, and there was an entrance to it from the south next to the western pillar of the southern row.

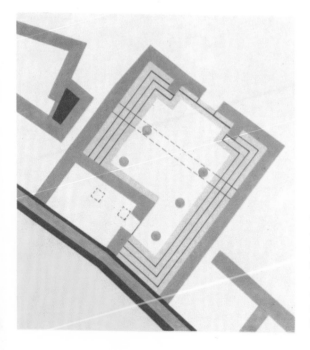

The synagogue went through various stages of use in its history. This plan shows it in its final stage with the bases of two columns of its original construction under the floor of the corner room.

Overleaf: An aerial view of the synagogue and the adjacent casemate wall, towards the end of the dig. The corner room was added by the Zealots and under its floor two scrolls were found.

Opposite: A comparison of two building phases of the synagogue: (*left*) the original Herodian building with (*right*) the Zealots' modifications. Note how two of the original columns were removed by the Zealots and placed on the foundations of the wall separating the entrance porch and the main hall.

Excavation of communal building, probably synagogue

Even while excavating we felt that the final stage, at least, of the building, and particularly the benches, had been constructed by the Zealots. Not only did we find many coins from the period of the revolt on the floor of this room, but here and there, where the plaster on the benches had peeled, we could tell that the benches had in fact been made out of quarried stone and broken pieces of dressed stone which had been taken from other buildings on Masada. Particularly conspicuous among these were portions of column drums and of capitals which could be identified immediately as having belonged to the lower and perhaps also to the upper terrace of the northern palace-villa. It was clear that at least these benches had been built after various parts of the palace-villa had been destroyed; and it was even clearer that this structure had the character of a communal building and was designed for public gatherings. But what was its purpose?

During the first season we already dared to suggest, albeit with considerable hesitation, that it was perhaps a synagogue. What strengthened this assumption was also the fact that the entrance faced east, and it was wholly oriented towards Jerusalem, as required by the traditional injunctions of the Sages. Moreover, we found on the floor an ostracon with the inscription 'Priestly tithe', that is, one of the tithes that was allocated to the Levites, and another inscribed sherd which bore the name 'Hezekiah', perhaps the name of a priest.

In one corner of the main room we found scores of soot-blackened lamps and in the rear cell the floor was covered with the remains of a powerful fire, and it was evident that numerous articles of furniture and many vessels had been collected here and set alight. They included handsome vessels of glass and metal, and among them was a wash-basin.

If what we had just unearthed was indeed a synagogue, then this was a discovery of front rank importance in the field of Jewish archaeology and certainly one of the most important finds in Masada. For up to then the very earliest synagogues discovered in Israel belonged to the end of the 2nd or beginning of the 3rd century AD. There were no remains of any synagogue from the period of the Second Temple.

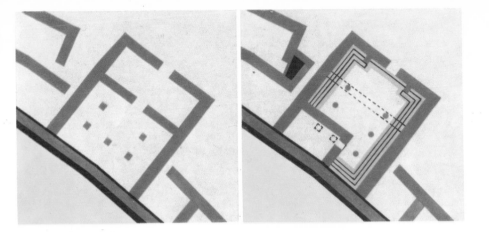

Because of its outstanding importance, we decided to continue our excavations of this building in the second season, and to cut sections in it and its vicinity to enable us to examine the stages of its construction. What spurred us particularly was the fact that towards the end of the first season, while cutting a section in the upper floor level of the rear cell, we found beneath it the base of an additional column. It was clear, however, that those who built the last floor of the building, while building this special cell in its corner, had removed that column and covered its base with the floor. It was evident therefore that before the Zealot stage of construction, the plan of the building had been different.

The cuts made during the second season showed that there had been two clear stages of construction: the last structure, with the benches, was as shown in the plan on the right; in its earlier stage, the building had an ante-room, and the main room had had columns along its southern, western and northern sides, as may be seen in the plan on the left. When the Zealots came to add the cell and the benches, they removed two of the pillars from the western row, tore down the wall dividing the ante-room from the main room to its west and set up the two pillars in its place.

It is difficult to determine the function of the building in the original Herodian plan, but one may hazard the guess that even then it served as a synagogue. The theory may be backed by the following assumptions. First, it seems most unlikely that Herod would have denied a place of worship for the Jewish members of his family and for other Jews who were members of his court. Second, the architectural plan with its pillars is very reminiscent of the plan of several early synagogues discovered in Galilee. And third, there exists a strong conservative tradition in the siting of houses of worship, and it would be in keeping with this tradition that the Zealots, when deciding on their synagogue, specifically chose this place knowing that it had previously served as a synagogue. This would explain, too, why even the original building had been oriented towards Jerusalem. It is possible that in the period between Herod and the Zealots, when Masada was occupied by the Roman garrison, the building may have served as a stable, for

Two stages of construction shown

Also a synagogue in the Herodian period

185

The place under the floor of the corner of the synagogue where the *Deuteronomy* scroll was found. On the left is the base of the column under the floor.

between the two floors, the original and the later one, we found many layers of animal dung.

I turn now to a most interesting find which, I believe, enables us to state with greater certainty that this building was indeed a synagogue. While making the exploratory cuts in the rear cell, the two architects of our expedition, Dunayevsky and Menzel, measured the distance between the bases of the two columns we found there and examined the filling between the two floors. In so doing they extended the area of the cut, and came upon a piece of a rolled scroll. (It was the first time, incidentally, that an architect at Masada had the fortune to find a scroll!) How had it got there, and why beneath the upper floor? When we studied the area of the cut more carefully, we found that a pit had once been dug at this spot, from the upper floor. The scroll was found at the bottom of this pit which had later been filled with earth and stones. This had therefore been a kind of *geniza* (where orthodox Jews buried – since they would not destroy – documents in the holy language, Hebrew, which had gone out of use, either because they were old and tattered or because they contained mistakes). This scroll may have been buried while the Zealots lived here because it was no longer usable, or it may have been hidden by them just before they ended their lives. Whichever it was, we were spurred by the find to excavate the whole of the upper floor in the rear cell to see if there were any other such pits.

Proof that structure was indeed a synagogue

In the picture opposite Chief Petty Officer Moshe Cohen, from the Israeli Navy, known colloquially as Mussa, is standing above the first cut where the scroll was found. (Mussa, incidentally, spent many months with our expedition and helped us greatly with safety measures when excavating dangerous sites on the edge of the heights.) To him I assigned the delicate task of clearing and sifting through the earth above the upper floor. After several days' work, he discovered a portion of the floor missing in the southern section of the cell, and beneath it a pit full of stamped down earth. At the very moment of his discovery, an urgent telegram arrived recalling Mussa to his job in the Navy for three days. He begged us to hold up the clearance work until his return, and though it was not easy to restrain our eagerness, we agreed to the delay. When he returned, he immediately resumed excavating the pit, while we all stood by tense with excitement. Within a few hours he had reached almost to the bottom of the pit and there his groping hands found the remains of a scroll. Though the parchment was badly gnawed, we could immediately identify the writing as chapters from the *Book of Ezekiel*; and the parts that were better preserved than others, and which we could easily read, contained extracts from Chapter 37 – the vision of the dry bones.

As for the rolled scroll discovered in the first pit, it was found on opening – which had to be done with great care in the laboratory in Jerusalem – to contain parts of the two final chapters of the *Book of Deuteronomy*. But the tightly rolled core of the scroll, on which we had pinned much hope, turned out to our dismay to be simply the blank end 'sheets' of the scroll. They had been sewn to the written 'sheets' to facilitate rolling and unrolling.

It need hardly be added at this stage that these two scrolls, too, are virtually identical with the traditional biblical texts. There are only a few slight changes in the *Ezekiel* scroll.

These two scrolls are important in themselves. They also lend support, *Date of scrolls* as we have indicated, to the probability that this building was indeed a synagogue. But there is another aspect of high importance to the discovery of these two scrolls: they are the only ones found not on the floor of a room but in a *geniza*, beneath the floor laid by the Zealots. This means that the date of the scrolls cannot possibly be later than 73 AD and not even the most sceptical of scholars can challenge this.

All in all, we discovered at Masada portions of fourteen scrolls, biblical, sectarian and apocryphal. From the point of view of scroll research and a study of the literature of the Second Temple period, these were the most important discoveries of our Masada excavations.

Apart from scrolls, other important inscriptions were found. These *Ostraca also found* were the ostraca, inscribed pieces of pottery, which was the common writing material for everyday use. Papyrus and parchment were too costly for such a purpose. Altogether we discovered almost 700 inscriptions on pottery. Where such inscriptions had been written on complete vessels, they are short, simply recording the name of the owner. The names we found were Jewish names, written in Hebrew, and most of them are familiar. Where the owner was a male, the inscription would contain both his and his father's names; where it was a woman, she would appear as the wife or the daughter of so-and-so. The inscription on one jug is worth mentioning. It read *Kahana Raba Aqavia*, the literal translation of which is 'Great Priest Aqavia'. What it meant was that the owner of the vessel was Aqavia, and he was *of the family* of High Priests.

We also found jars belonging to the Herodian period. They were almost all broken vessels, and it is possible that the Zealots forebore from using them. From the archaeological point of view, these sherds were of great importance, enabling us to observe with ease the differences in the shapes and makes of pottery vessels that had developed from the period of Herod to that of the Zealots, only a brief – in archaeological terms – seventy years. In this sphere, we were extremely lucky to find sherds of wine jars which *Dated sherds of* bore an exact date – a very rare and always hoped for occurrence at *wine-jar found* an archaeological dig. The dating on these jars followed the standard Roman system of date recording – by noting the name of the consul of that particular year. In our case, all the jars bore the name of the Roman consul for the year 19 BC, C. Sentius Saturninus. These jars had contained wine which had been specially sent from Italy to Herod. We know this from the last line of the inscription, which read: 'To King Herod of Judea'. This was the first time we had discovered an inscription with the name of Herod.

Among the various ostraca were quite a number with a specific type of *Interesting ostraca* inscription – a name accompanied by a special sign. There were three groups of this type of ostraca: on the sherds of the first group appeared the

Opposite: Portions of the *Ezekiel* scroll, containing the vision of the 'dry bones', which were found in the second pit under the floor of the synagogue.

189

Three of the special ostraca which may have been coupons or passes.
Top: the name 'Yehohanan', a Greek *Alpha* and *Yod* in Paleo-Hebrew script.
Bottom left: the name 'Yehuda', *Samekh* in Paleo-Hebrew script on right and a
Greek *Beta* written from right to left. *Bottom right:* the name 'Shimeon',
Gimel on right and *Daleth* in Paleo-Hebrew script.

name *Yehohanan* (John), written literally in the handwriting of the man –
his signature in fact. Below it, to the left, was the letter *Alpha* (A), and to
the right the letter *Yod* (Y) in the Paleo-Hebrew script. The second group
bore the name *Shimeon* (Simon), below it the letter *Gimel* (G) and to its left
the letter *Daleth* (D) or perhaps *Resh* (R) also in the Paleo-Hebrew script.
Here, too, *Shimeon* appeared as a signature. The third group of sherds
contained the name *Yehuda* (Judah), and below it the letter *Samekh* (S) in
Paleo-Hebrew, and the Greek letter *Beta*, written from right to left instead
of from left to right.

What were these ostraca? Were they some kind of coupon or chit? And
for what were they used? The combination of name and symbol suggests a
conventional sign or perhaps an esoteric code. For what purpose? Can it be
that John, Simon and Judah were the names of commanders, or of brigades,
and that the troops of the particular unit were given these 'chits' to draw
their rations? Or perhaps they were 'passes' to enable them to enter the
Masada stronghold? Or was this whole system of 'chits' associated with the
distribution of the special rations for priests and Levites? We can only
speculate; we have no definitive answer.

There were some 275 ostraca of another type, where each sherd bore a

Various ostraca with Hebrew letters on them;
hundreds of these were found.

single letter, two letters or three; and again we have no way of knowing
what this meant. The lettering, I may say, is done in a very beautiful
script. We found ostraca with such markings as the Hebrew for '*Z*', '*ZZ*',
'*ZZZ*', '*QA*', '*GT*', and indeed almost all the letters of the Hebrew alphabet
are represented. The bulk of these sherds were found near the storehouses,
so perhaps they had something to do with the rationing system of the
Zealots during the siege.

It is clear that the writing on the ostraca was done by experienced
scribes, and these inscriptions fill gaps in our knowledge of writing during
the period of the Second Temple. Though very short, these inscriptions are
of great palaeographic value and shed much light on the history of Hebrew
script. In the case of the scrolls, we were aided by the archaeological and
historical data in determining that they could not be later than 73 AD, but
we could not know exactly when they had actually been copied, for each
scroll may have been in the possession of its owner for decades. With the
ostraca, however, it was possible to be accurate to within seven years, and to
determine with absolute certainty that those with the Hebrew inscriptions
were written between 66 and 73 AD, namely, the period when Masada was
occupied by the Zealots.

*Inscriptions of great
palaeographic value*

15 The remains of the last defenders

The defenders of Masada, as testified by Josephus, died by their own hands. The exceptions were two women and several children who hid themselves during the suicide operation and who later recounted to the conquering Roman unit what had taken place in Masada in the final moments. From the very beginning of our excavation we concerned ourselves with the problem of finding the remains of the defenders – whether there were such remains and if so where they were likely to be. The probability that they would be found was dim indeed. According to Josephus, General Silva established a Roman garrison on the Masada summit after its conquest, a fact confirmed by our excavations, and it could be assumed that this garrison would have disposed of the bodies in one way or another for sanitary reasons. Nevertheless we retained the hope that we might perhaps find some, and from the very outset we were on the search for possible places where they might have lain unnoticed. We did find three skeletons on the lower terrace of the palace-villa, as has been mentioned, and they were almost certainly those of the final Jewish defenders. Would we come across others?

Search for remains of defenders of Masada

One of the sites where it seemed probable that we might find skeletons of bodies buried or thrown by the Roman garrison was the network of caves near the top of the southern cliff of the Masada rock, only a few yards below the casemate wall. There had apparently been some early intention of using these caves to store water. (Next to them are two of the largest among the upper cisterns of Masada.) But apparently some of them were found unsuitable for this purpose and the project was abandoned. Our excavations showed that some of Masada's defenders dwelt in these caves at various times, as indicated by remains of food and domestic utensils which we found. And it was in one of the smaller of these caves that we came upon the stark sight of skulls and other parts of skeletons scattered in disorder about the floor. Among the bones were fragments of linen and pieces of clothing. A brief examination showed that there were altogether about twenty-five skeletons. Had these been the bodies of Zealots? Had they been troops of the Roman garrison? Or had they been the monks of the Byzantine Period? At the time we could give no accurate opinion. But now, after the bones have been carefully studied by my colleague Dr N. Hass, of the Hebrew University Medical School, the following facts have

Discovery of a group of skeletons

Opposite: Searching for caves on the southern cliff above the cave with skeletons – looking east. The Roman camp is below and nearby the modern hostel.

The southern cliff of Masada showing the caves below the casemate wall.
Skeletons were found in the small cave on the left. See pages 198–9.

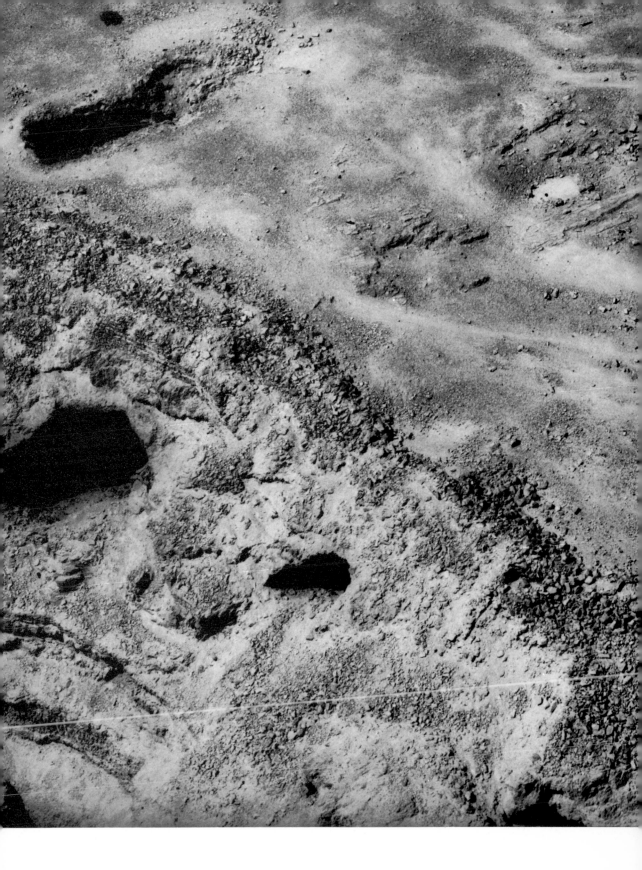

Plaits and sandals as they were found. Compare with the picture on page 56.

been established: fourteen of the skeletons are of males between the ages of twenty-two and sixty; one is of a man over the age of seventy; six are females aged between fifteen and twenty-two; and four are children aged from eight to twelve; there is also one of an embryo! Most of the skulls belong to the same type as those we discovered in the Caves of Bar Kochba in Nahal Hever. It seems to me that these facts conclusively rule out the possibility that the skeletons are those either of the Roman garrison or of the monks. They can be only those of the defenders of Masada.

Could they have been thrown into this cave by their own comrades during the siege? This is difficult to believe. The only feasible assumption is that they were flung here irreverently by the Roman troops when they cleared the bodies after their victory.

In no other place on Masada did we find additional skeletons. In our search, we made several exploratory sectional-cuts in places where such finds seemed likely, but without success. It is possible that we may have missed some pit where bodies might have been cast, but I think that on the whole our excavations confirmed our earlier view that the Roman garrison which occupied Masada for several decades after the dramatic event cleared the area of all such human remains. Thus, apart from the twenty-five skeletons found in the cave and possibly the three found in the palace-villa, no physical remains of the last defenders of Masada were left. But the moving words of Josephus have kept them alive to this day:

For the husbands tenderly embraced their wives and took their children into their arms, and gave the longest parting kisses to them, with tears in their eyes. Yet at the same time did they complete what they had resolved on, as if they had been executed by the hands of strangers, and they had nothing else for their comfort but the necessity they were in of doing this execution, to avoid that prospect they had of the misery they were to suffer from their enemies.

At every archaeological excavation, there is always at least one visitor who, after being shown all the digging sites and the finds, asks: 'Well, what was your most important discovery?' This, for me, is a difficult question to answer, for every archaeological find has its own special importance. The structures, the wall-paintings, the mosaics – all are of great value for a study of Herodian period architecture, the nature of Masada, and the character of King Herod. The coins and the ostraca are of considerable importance for certain paleographic and historical studies. The thousands of pottery sherds and stone vessels, articles of leather and straw, cosmetic vials, jewellery, the ovens and cooking stoves, the ritual baths (*mikves*), the synagogue, and especially the scrolls – these are invaluable for research into the Jewish archaeology of the Second Temple period.

If, however, I were pressed to single out one discovery more spectacular than any other, I would point to a find which may not be of the greatest importance from the point of view of pure archaeology, but which certainly, when we came upon it, electrified everyone in Masada who was engaged in the dig, professional archaeologist and lay volunteer alike.

197

The skeletons in the cave were found with the bones in this disorder.

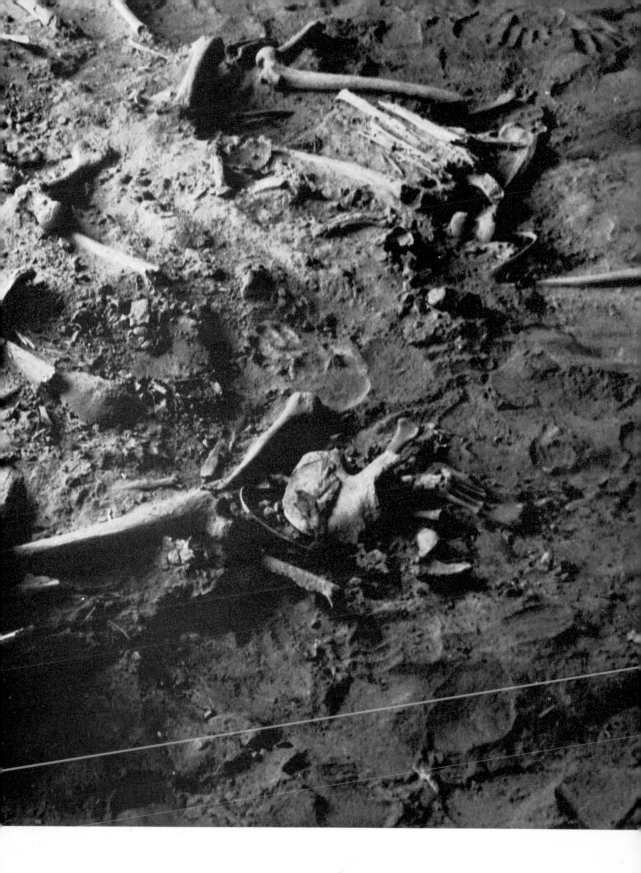

A typical sight in the public buildings of Masada: charred
beams and ashes, seen here in one of the storerooms.

This find was in one of the most strategic spots on Masada, close to the gate which leads to the 'water path' and near the square between the storehouses and the administration building where all the northern tracks on the summit meet. The debris on this site was being cleared by a group of volunteers – one of whom, incidentally, is an elephant-tamer in civilian life – when they came across eleven, small, strange ostraca, different from any other which had come to light in Masada. Upon each was inscribed a single name, each different from its fellow, though all appeared to have been written by the same hand. The names themselves were also odd, rather like nicknames, as for example 'Man from the valley' or *Yoav* ('Joab'). ('Joab' may seem perfectly ordinary, but it was extremely rare during the period of the Second Temple, and it was almost certainly applied to a man who was particularly brave.)

As we examined these ostraca, we were struck by the extraordinary thought: 'Could it be that we had discovered evidence associated with the death of the very last group of Masada's defenders?' Josephus writes, in a passage immediately following the one we have just quoted:

Possible evidence of last group of defenders

> They then chose ten men by lot out of them, to slay all the rest; everyone of whom laid himself down by his wife and children on the ground, and threw his arms about them and they offered their necks to the stroke of those who by lot executed that melancholy office; and when these ten had, without fear, slain them all, they made the same rule for casting lots for themselves, that he whose lot it was to first kill the other nine, and after all, should kill himself.

Had we indeed found the very ostraca which had been used in the casting of the lots? We shall never know for certain. But the probability is strengthened by the fact that among these eleven inscribed pieces of pottery was one bearing the name 'Ben Ya'ir'. The inscription of plain 'Ben Ya'ir' on Masada at that particular time could have referred to no other than Eleazar ben Ya'ir. And it also seems possible that this final group were his ten commanders who had been left to the last, after the decision had been wholly carried out, and who had then cast lots amongst themselves.

A concluding word about Ben Ya'ir and about a frequent sight in various parts of Masada throughout our excavations – the remains of the dreadful fires, the fires that accompanied the heroes of Masada in their death.

It is thanks to Ben Ya'ir and his comrades, to their heroic stand, to their choice of death over slavery, and to the burning of their humble chattels as a final act of defiance to the enemy, that they elevated Masada to an undying symbol of desperate courage, a symbol which has stirred hearts throughout the last nineteen centuries. It is this which moved scholars and laymen to make the ascent to Masada. It is this which moved the modern Hebrew poet to cry: 'Masada shall not fall again!' It is this which has drawn the Jewish youth of our generation in their thousands to climb to its summit in a solemn pilgrimage. And it is this which brings the recruits of the armoured units of the Defence Forces of modern Israel to swear the oath of allegiance on Masada's heights: 'Masada shall not fall again!'

The name 'Ben Ya'ir' written on one of the eleven sherds. Ben Ya'ir is most probably Eleazar ben Ya'ir, commander of the Zealots at Masada.

Masada and Israel today

Recruits of the armoured unit of the Israeli Defence Forces
swearing the oath of allegiance on top of Masada.

The set of stamps issued by the Israeli Post-Office to commemorate the excavations.

The two sides of the special medal struck by the Israeli Government.

Historical and archaeological chart

Period	Date	The finds
Chalcolithic	4th millenium	Caves in cliffs
First Temple	10th to 7th centuries BC	Scattered sherds
Hasmonean	103–40 BC	Coins of Alexander Janneus
Herod the Great	40–4 BC	Fortress, palaces, storerooms, bath-house, water cisterns, coins
Dynasty of Herod and Procurators	4 BC–AD 66	Hundreds of coins, additions to buildings
The Great Revolt	AD 66–73	Dwellings, ritual baths, synagogue, scrolls, ostraca, coins and articles of daily use
After the Revolt	AD 73–111	Coins of the Roman garrison, some additional buildings
Byzantine	5th–6th centuries AD	Chapel, monks' cells

16 Masada's history in the light of the finds

In the course of our two-season, eleven months' dig, we excavated 97 per cent of the built-on area of Masada. Though this does not mean that we now know all there is to know of the secrets of Masada, we have learned enough from the archaeological discoveries to present the main events in its history.

Archaeological evidence for the history of Masada

The earliest known occupants of the site, as revealed by our dig, belonged to the Chalcolithic period – fourth millenium B.C. We unearthed their remains in a small cave on the lower part of the southern cliff, remains of plants, cloth, mats and sherds of Chalcolithic pottery found in 'cup-marks' on the floor. It is not to be concluded from these remains that their owners were a settled community established on Masada. They were one of the scores of typical cave-dwelling communities who lived in the Judean desert in that period.

Pottery finds date earliest occupants

In several places, including the middle terrace of the northern palace-villa, we found a few scattered sherds from the time of the Israelite monarchy. We found no building which could be ascribed to this period, and it may therefore be assumed that these sherds simply show that from time to time during this era a few isolated individuals sojourned there.

One of the purposes of our expedition was to find the buildings erected, according to Josephus, by 'Jonathan the High Priest' – to find them, determine their date and identify the 'Jonathan'. We were only partially successful in our search for the solution. We discovered no structure which could with certainty be attributed to any period before that of Herod. Moreover, none of our pottery finds could be said to match the pre-Herodian types. On the other hand, we discovered scores of coins struck by Alexander Janneus (among them the most ancient of all the coins found at Masada). We can therefore now say, perhaps, that any buildings and cisterns, which were constructed on this site in the period before King Herod, were the work of King Alexander Janneus, and he is probably the 'Jonathan the High Priest' mentioned by Josephus.

Who was 'Jonathan the High Priest'?

If we were partially unsuccessful, however, in unravelling this problem, we were highly successful in unearthing every building erected by Herod: his palaces, his service structures and his fortifications. It is now definitely established that the Masada of King Herod was basically a citadel bounded by a casemate wall. In its western section stood his large palace with its residential, ceremonial and administrative functions; at its northern edge, just beneath the wall, perched his private palace-villa. In addition to these, Herod built several small palaces for members of his family and for his high officials. Most of the northern sector of the summit is taken up with the long and narrow storerooms, the large public baths, the administration building and the 'apartment' building.

To complete this Herodian picture, mention should be made of the amazing water system, whereby flash-flood water from the wadis was channelled through aqueducts to two series of huge cisterns which had been scooped out of the rock on the north-western slope of Masada. These cisterns were not among the sites excavated by our expedition.

Between the period of Herod and that of the great revolt of the Jews against the Romans, Masada had been a site of continuous settlement. This was known from Josephus who reported that the Roman garrison there was destroyed when Masada was captured by Menahem at the beginning of the Jewish revolt. Although we were unable to find any buildings which could definitely be ascribed to this period, our excavations confirmed such settlement, the most convincing of our finds being the hundreds of coins from the reign of Archilaus and of Agrippa, and particularly from the rule of the various Procurators (Roman governors).

As for the Masada of the Zealots, we can summarise our findings by stating that their main dwellings were in the chambers of the casemate wall, in which partition walls, stoves and cupboards had been installed. When these proved inadequate to meet the housing needs of the newcomers, additional dwellings were built, most of them close to the casemate wall. Several of the palaces also served as living quarters, possibly for the commanders. During this period, almost no additional public buildings were erected: to house their workshops and bakeries they used the wall towers. However, they did add some structures for special functions, mostly religious, such as ritual baths, a religious school and synagogue, but even there for the most part they utilised earlier buildings. Some Herodian structures, like the storehouses, were used by the Zealots as they were, without alteration, for they suited their needs. Some, like the palace-villa and the purely decorative parts of other buildings, such as ornamental columns, were not needed for their original functions, and so for example, sections of these columns were utilised for buildings they did need – the southern *mikve*, the synagogue benches, tables, and so forth – and as general building material. And fancy wooden floors were pulled up and used as fuel, particularly in the final phase of the siege before the Roman breach. It appears that parts of the palace-villa were already in a state of disrepair when the Zealots occupied Masada.

The large collection of 'pennies' (*prutot*) – bronze coins – of the period of the revolt, which we found mainly in the buildings used by the public, such as the southern *mikve*, the northern storehouses, the western palace, and the bakeries, suggests that life on Masada at this time was organised on a communal basis with centralised planning and control. These coins and the ostraca may therefore have been used as coupons or chits for a system of food rationing and the administration of services for the whole community.

All the public buildings which we excavated bore signs of having been burned in a formidable conflagration, matching the description in Josephus. Similar signs were evident in some of the Zealotian dwellings, where we found heaps of ashes in corners of the rooms with remains of humble family possessions.

Burning confirms description by Josephus

On the Roman occupation of Masada after the revolt, Josephus observes that General Silva left a garrison there, but he does not give details of its size nor of its length of stay. Today we can say that Masada was garrisoned by the Romans for at least forty years. This we know from the coins we found both on the summit and in the large Roman camp at its western foot. This was Silva's camp, whose inner section was built after the conquest, as our dig revealed.

Of the Byzantine period, our excavations show that the monks who established themselves on Masada did so after the powerful earthquake which shook the area and caused great destruction to many of the buildings on the summit. The foundations of cells and other structures built by the Byzantine monks were found high up, resting on mounds of rubble and stones which covered the remains of the Roman garrison and the last defenders of Masada. To the future archaeologist is left the excavation of the Roman camps and clearance of the huge water cisterns. This may be done one day.

Byzantine occupation after earthquake

Silva's camp F is in the bottom right of this aerial view of Masada looking
south-east. Above it is the small camp E with part of the circumvallation.
The Roman ramp is clearly visible in the middle of the western part of Masada.

17 The other side of the hill

We have devoted almost this entire survey to an account of the Masada fortress, confining ourselves to the rock itself, its buildings, its fortifications, its last defenders, without touching much on its surroundings. This we have done not only because of the central archaeological interest in the remains on the summit, nor only out of admiration for the heroism of the Zealots, but primarily because this is the story of our archaeological dig, and this was limited to the mount of Masada and did not take in its environs.

There is, however, no more impressive testimony to the courage of the defenders than the remains of the Roman camps and their siege structures which surround Masada. These also show that the Romans well appreciated the difficulties they could expect in trying to capture the fortress with its 960 Zealots. The Roman remains are in a fine state of preservation, due partly to the dryness of the desert but also to their remoteness throughout the centuries from centres of settlement whose people would have been happy to raid them for building materials. These remains represent one of the finest examples of siege works in the whole of the Roman empire.

The camps have not yet been subjected to an archaeological dig, though one has been partly excavated and restored by Shmaryahu Guttman. The plan of the camps, on the other hand, was investigated in a basic way by the well-known archaeologists Schulten, Hawkes, Richmond and others. They were able to do this without excavating, thanks to the excellent state of the camps; their general layout, too, showed up well in aerial photographs. Our own expedition carried out a small dig in one of the camps, not to find out anything about its plan but only to learn the types of pottery vessels used by the Roman army and compare them with the pottery we found on the Masada summit which belonged to the Roman garrison after the conquest. We are in no position, therefore, to add, from personal investigation, to the description of the Roman siege works which resulted from the earlier researches.

Siege works around Masada only briefly investigated

Yet these researches, for all their importance, are still far from satisfactory. This is mainly due to the very short time these scholars were able to devote to their subject in the field, which is why, for example, Schulten, Richmond and Guttman can come up with three different plans of the same camp (camp A). It is evident, when there are such glaring discrepancies between the three, that the true original plan of the Roman camps may be

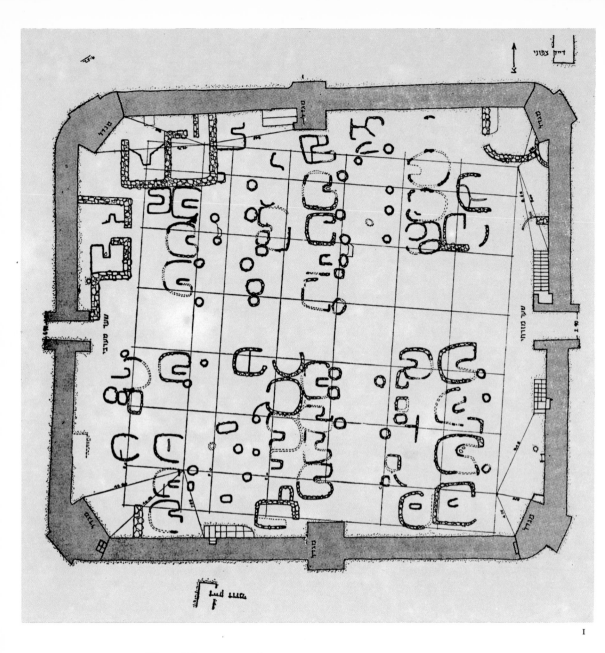

I

Plans of Roman camp A.
1 Guttman's plan.
2 Richmond's plan.
3 Schulten's plan.

Lager A

1 : 500

2

3

discovered only after a detailed excavation. Nevertheless, the general picture of the Roman military effort is sufficiently clear, and the writings of Josephus explain and complement what may be seen on the ground today.

In this outline, we shall begin with the camps and the siege wall, and end with the structures built to make possible the breach and the assault. This is what Josephus had to say about the Roman 'side of the hill':

When Bassus [the procurator] was dead in Judea, Flavius Silva succeeded him as a procurator there; who, when he saw that all the rest of the country was subdued in this war, and that there was but one only stronghold that was still in rebellion, he got all his army together that lay in different places, and made an expedition against it. This fortress was Masada . . . The Roman general came, and led his army against Eleazar and those Sicarii who held the fortress Masada together with him; and for the whole country adjoining, he presently gained it, and put garrisons into the most proper places of it; he also built a wall quite round the entire fortress, that none of the besieged might easily escape: he also set his men to guard the several parts of it; he also pitched his camp in such an agreeable place as he had chosen for the siege, and at which place the rock belonging to the fortress did make the nearest approach to the neighbouring mountain, which yet was a place of difficulty for getting plenty of provisions; for it was not only food that was to be brought from a great distance and this with great deal of pain to those [prisoners] Jews who were appointed for that purpose, but water was also to be brought to the camp, because the place afforded no fountain that was near it . . .

Overleaf: The camps are marked on this general view of Masada; north is at the left of the picture.

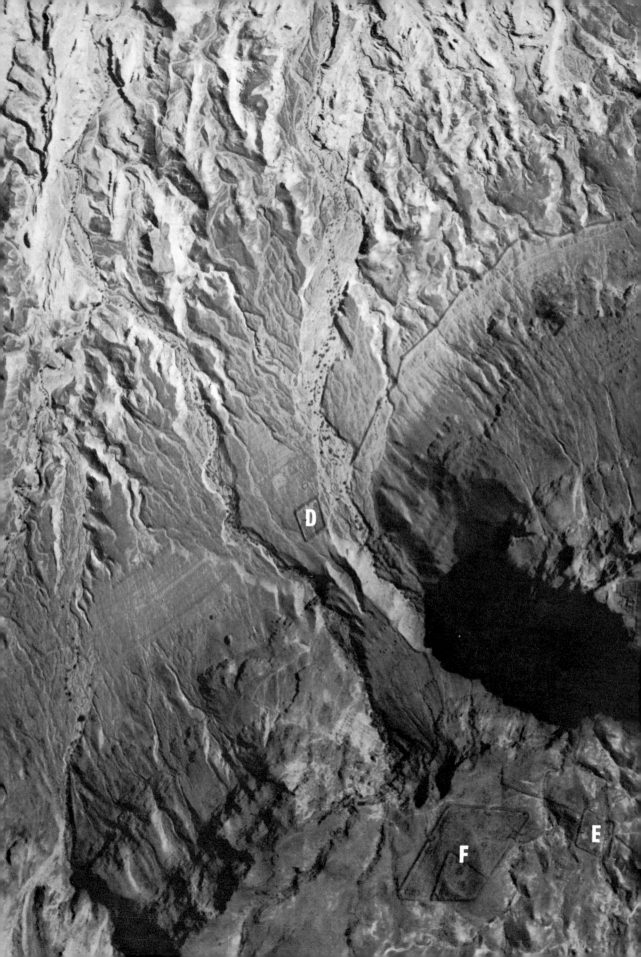

(When I read this extract from Josephus on the problem of supplies, I thought how closely it resembled the troubles we had with our expedition in setting up our own camp.)

Plan of siege works indicates purpose of the Roman general

These words of Josephus underline the basic plan of General Silva and the problems he faced. But before describing the siege works, we must ask ourselves the question: what was Silva's military aim? And was he forced to change it in the course of the engagement? In other words, did Silva believe he would subdue Masada's defenders by siege? Was it his intention to capture only the fortress? Or was it his purpose, come what may, to capture all the beleaguered persons, dead or alive?

It seems to me that the words of Josephus and the plan of the camps and siege works leave no room for doubt on these matters. Silva well knew that the defenders of Masada were among the most daring, zealous and desperate people who had ever stood up to and resisted the Roman army. Moreover, he cannot have thought that a siege would bring them to their knees for he knew that, quite apart from their fighting qualities, they had considerable quantities of water and food on the summit. To subjugate them through siege would have taken a very long time indeed, and this Silva could not permit himself, if only because of the climatic conditions. He had to complete the conquest of Masada before the onset of the burning summer. It therefore follows from all this, that Silva planned an assault on the fortress from the very outset.

Masada challenged the entire might of Rome

If this is so, however, why did he expend so much energy and resources in encircling Masada with a siege wall of more than 3,800 yards? The answer is given by Josephus, in the extract we have just quoted: the wall was built to prevent the escape of the beleaguered defenders, and this, without doubt, was Silva's principal purpose. For all the strategic importance of the fortress Masada for the Roman army, the fact is that what disturbed the tranquillity of the Roman empire were the 960 men, women and children holding out on its summit. Judea had been vanquished. In Rome they had triumphantly installed their arches of triumph. And here, in this place alone (after the conquest of Herodion and Machaeros), there remained a handful of rebels challenging the entire might of Rome. This they considered a double danger. The rebels could use Masada as a base for forays against centres of settlement and units of the Roman army. Perhaps more important, by their very existence the Zealots could spark anew the embers of the rebellion which in fact were smouldering all the time – as witness the revolt of Bar Kochba which broke out sixty years after the fall of Masada. One can well imagine the stern and urgent orders from Titus in Rome to Silva in Palestine, commanding him to liquidate the 'nest of rebels' at all cost and without delay. And it is surely no accident that the conquest of Masada was not celebrated in Rome, or at all events found no mention in the Roman annals of that time. In the Roman records, after all, Judea had been captured three years earlier, and *Judaea Capta* coins were already in circulation.

The powerful effort put into the construction of the siege wall (circum-

Roman coin with the inscription 'Judaea Capta' showing a Roman
legionary and a captive Jewish woman under a palm tree.

vallation) round Masada – even built on parts of the slopes which any way
were almost unnegotiable – arouses our wonder to this day. Already six
feet thick, its eastern section was further fortified by twelve towers built at
intervals of 80 to 100 yards. No less impressive are the eight camps at
various points round the base of the fortress. So well are they preserved that
from the air or from the edge of the Masada summit, they look today as
though they had just been abandoned. The camps had a triple function:
quarters for the troops; domination of possible escape routes from the
summit; defence of the troops themselves against surprise raids. The size
and locations of the camps were fixed in accordance with these tasks. There
were two large camps and six small ones. The large ones are B in the east
and F in the west. Both were outside the circumvallation, which lay
between them and the fortress. Camp B is 140 by 180 yards and F is 130 by
160 yards. Both are very similar in size and plan to the classic camp of the
Roman legions, and there is little doubt that they were manned by the
main strength of the Tenth Legion (*Fretensis*) itself, about half in B and half
in F. From the report of Josephus, it can be taken that Silva's own command
headquarters were located in camp F.

*Location of the
Roman camps*

This camp stands slightly to the north of and close to the assault ramp,
and from this vantage point Silva could not only follow the course of battle
with ease, but he could also, if he was so minded, speak directly with
Eleazar! (The acoustics here are so clear that from the top of Masada we
could speak to the team excavating some of the rooms of this camp.) We

The large camp B, situated east of Masada.
(The bus is on the metal road leading to the hostel.)

can well imagine the exchange of curses and mutual vilification in the 'psychological warfare' that must have gone on between besieger and besieged on this sector of the front.

This camp poses a special problem for archaeologists. In its north-western corner there was a smaller camp (F2) strengthened by towers. In the course of its construction, parts of the large camp were destroyed, which indicates clearly that it was built at a later date. Scholars are divided as to its period. Some hold that it housed the Roman garrison immediately after the fall of Masada. Others argue that it is very much later, and was part of the network of *limes Palestineae* in the days of Diocletian, about 300 A D.

Pottery and coins help to date Camp F

As I have mentioned, we carried out a small dig in camp F for its pottery, but since we were there we also looked for signs which would shed light on the date of construction of F2. What we found proved conclusively

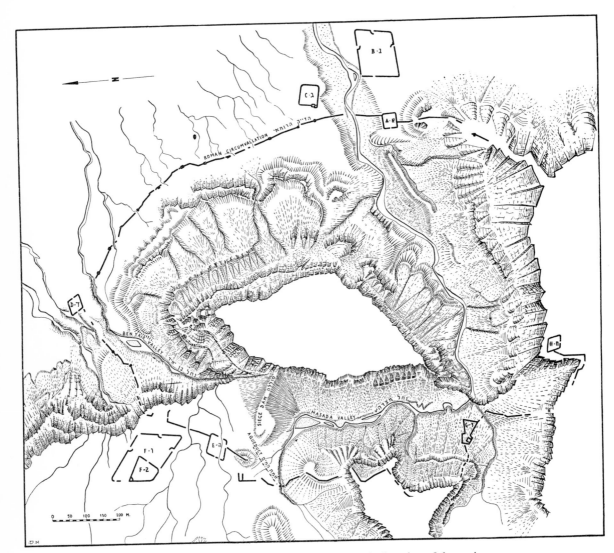

A plan of Masada and its vicinity showing the location of the various camps, the circumvallation and the aqueduct of the Herodian water system.

that it was used by the Roman garrison which was left there after Masada fell. The pottery and coins found there all belong to the last decades of the 1st century and the beginning of the 2nd century AD.

Both large camps, F and B, are similar and have four gates, one in each of the four sides, which gave entry to the two roads inside the camp: the east-west road was the headquarters road (*via praetoria*) and the north-south road was the troop commander's road (*via principalis*). In the classic Roman camps the names given to these four gates were *porta praetoria* (front gate) and *porta decumana* (rear gate) – named after the tenth unit of the legion which was encamped there – which stood at either end of the *via praetoria*; and *porta principalis dextra* (right gate) and *porta principalis sinistra* (left gate).

General plan of camps

These gates were protected by inner barrier walls (*claviculae*). These walls turned inwards from the entrance, in contrast to the camps of Hadrian in the time of Bar Kochba where they were built outwards, as discovered in the camps near Nahal Hever.

It was possible to determine exactly, particularly from camp B, the principal buildings and their location in the centre of the camps: the command post (*praetorium*) with its large central court which had a re-fectory (*triclinium*) to hold twelve people who sat on stone couches arranged in three sides of a square; places of worship and ceremonials; the dais (*tribunal*), a square of three by three yards and one yard high, with a ramp where the commander stood when taking parades and addressing his troops; the altars (*arae*) for the Legion's sacrifices; the 'bird observatory' (*auguratorium*) from which the priests of the camp could determine the good and bad omens by watching the flight of birds, or the stars. These camps also boasted a market-place (*forum*) and treasury (*quaestorium*).

The most striking feature in these camps (and in the small ones too) were the hundreds of 'mess-units' (*contubernia*), each accommodating eight to nine soldiers. They were really bases for tents, and what has re-mained of these 'mess-units' and may be seen on the site today are low walls of rubble stone, about three to four-and-a-half feet high. These served as an upright foundation over which the tent was spread. The tent itself was kept up by its poles. In the climatic conditions of Masada, this system more or less solved the problem of troops' quarters. But the ex-perience of our own expedition shows that they must have suffered a good deal from time to time when the area was struck by winter storms. More-over, in accordance with Roman army custom, their camps were usually sited on the slope of the hill, and so they were not always able to avoid the force of flash-floods. Each tent had its sleeping and eating arrangements. The interior was mostly built in the form of a *triclinium* – stone benches on which the soldiers slept and sat during meals. In some parts of camp F where we dug, we found several *triclinia* which were very well preserved. Food was cooked near the tent, and we unearthed the remains of fire-places in their vicinity. The small camps differ from the two large ones also in their siting. All, except camp C, are linked to the circumvallation, and there

Airview towards west,
showing camp F and
the smaller inner
camp F2 at top right;
to its left, camp E.

221

can be no doubt that their main function was to serve as a kind of guard-camp both to cover the circumvallation (and prevent any attempted escape across it) and all surrounding features of any tactical importance.

The task of camp A was to bar possible passage through Wadi Sebbeh (Nahal Masada). This was also true of camp D which guarded the exit from Wadi Nimrein (Nahal Ben Ya'ir). Camp C, the only small camp outside the siege wall, like the two large ones, almost certainly was there to guard the beginning stretch of the 'snake path'; it is possible, too, that because of the nature of the terrain here, it was sited further away from the circumvallation and closer to camp B, so that it could also give protection to this large camp – just as camp E gave protection to camp F. Camp E, apart from this, and apart also from guarding the western approach, was sited on the most strategic spot of Masada, from the besiegers' point of view. It was possible from this spot to prevent the beleaguered defenders from going down to the two series of cisterns cut in the western slope and drawing their water. The siting of camps G and H seems odd at first glance; but after our excavations on the summit the reason is clear. As we indicated

One of the Roman tents after excavation, showing benches.

when dealing with the southern sector of the casemate wall, we found that from the southern edge it was possible in emergency to descend from or climb up to the fortress. Camp G was so located (in the south-west) that it could prevent such an operation. Camp H was established on the top of the promontory south of Wadi Sebbeh (Nahal Massada), exactly opposite the southern edge of Masada. From there it was possible even to see what was happening on the summit and it was thus an excellent look-out post for the entire southern sector.

In each of these camps A, D, G and H it was possible to quarter five *centuriae* of auxiliary troops, making a total altogether of about 2,000 men. Camps C and E could each hold almost 1,000. Thus, the built camps alone could house almost 9,000 troops, including the legion. But there is no doubt that the entire besieging force was very much larger, probably reaching 15,000 men if we add to the fighting units the thousands of Jewish prisoners who, according to Josephus, were used to bring water and food and apparently also to work on construction.

Hanging round the Roman camps were a mixed bag of 'camp-followers'

A view of camps A (*right*), B (*centre*) and C (*left*) from an excavated room of the eastern wall. The basalt mortar in the picture was actually found in this room.

223

A fragment of a Nabatean bowl of the kind found both
on top of Masada and in the Roman camps.

and tradesmen. The remains of their shacks may be seen very well in the
vicinity of the camps, particularly near camps E and F, where some of
them have two or three rooms. Apparently here too they used tents on
foundations of stone walls. We found large quantities of Nabatean pottery *Nabatean pottery*
in the remains of these buildings, as well as in the camps. It may therefore be *found*
assumed that many of the tradesmen were Nabateans and also, possibly,
that Nabateans constituted part of the auxiliary force. This is supported by
the fact that their vessels were found in the small camps and also in the
quarters of the Roman garrison on the Masada summit. (Discovery of their
pottery, incidentally, is of considerable archaeological importance, showing
conclusively that these vessels, even in their classical style, continued in use
right up to the seventies of the 1st century A D.)

With the building of the circumvallation, which was erected after the
construction of the camps, General Silva completed the first stage of his
plan. He was now arrayed for attack, with the defenders on Masada sealed
in tight.

Opposite: The dominant position of camp H over the southern portion
of Masada is very clear from this air view looking north.

The ramp (assault embankment)

The ramp built as an assault embankment by the Romans on the western slope of Masada, rising towards the casemate wall just north of its west gate, is undoubtedly one of the most remarkable siege structures of the Roman army which exists in the world today. It is in a good state of preservation. This is what Josephus had to say about it:

Since therefore the Roman commander Silva had now built a wall on the outside, round about this whole place, as we have said already, and had thereby made a most accurate provision to prevent any one of the besieged running away, he undertook the siege itself, though he found but one single place that would admit of the banks he was to raise; for behind that tower which secured the road that led to the palace, and to the top of the hill from the west, there was a certain eminency of the rock, very broad and very prominent, but three hundred cubits [= c 500 feet] beneath the highest part of Masada; it was called the 'White Promontory'. Accordingly he got upon that part of the rock, and ordered the army to bring earth; and when they fell to that work with alacrity, and abundance of them together, the bank was raised and became solid for two hundred cubits [= c 330 feet] in height yet was not this bank thought sufficiently high for the use of the engines that were to be set upon it; but still another elevated work of great stones compacted together was raised upon the bank; this was fifty cubits, both in breadth and height.

And, indeed, all who visit Masada are struck by the whiteness of the ramp, much of whose earth was taken from the 'white promontory' which may be seen in the area today on the exact site described by Josephus.

Josephus' account of measurements correct The measurements reported by Josephus are most accurate, if he was taking the height of the western edge of Masada as the distance between the summit at this point and the bottom of the dry river bed below. In fact, the distance between the base of the ramp and the casemate wall is about eighty yards. As may be seen today, the top of the ramp does not quite reach the wall, ending about twenty yards below it. This, too, matches the description of Josephus. The length of the ramp is some 215 yards, and its width at its broadest part, near the fortress, is about the same.

The ascent to the summit of Masada today is most easily made across this ramp, at the top of which a narrow footpath has been laid. As you climb this path you notice on the left an outcrop of timber tips protruding from the white earth. These are certainly the slats of the wooden support scaffolding used to prevent the earth from collapsing during the construction of the ramp. Of the high platform which was built at the top of the ramp, nothing remains today. It must have disintegrated long ago, its stones rolling down into the wadi below.

The powerful work and elements which went into the construction of the

Opposite: The view of the Roman ramp from the top of Masada. The expedition camp is in the top left corner of the picture and the cable is that of the expedition ferry.

Aerial view looking
south-east on comple-
tion of the excavations;
the Roman ramp (on
the right) almost
reaches the summit.

229

assault embankment enabled a high siege-tower to be established at the top of it, and a battering ram to be brought up which had a superstructure with additional catapults. This is what Josephus says about these siege instruments:

> The other machines that were now got ready were like to those that had been first devised by Vespasian, and afterwards Titus, for sieges. There was also a tower made of the height of sixty cubits, and all over plated with iron, out of which the Romans threw darts and stones from the engines, and soon made those that fought from the walls of the place to retire, and would not let them lift up their heads above the works. At the same time, Silva ordered that the great battering-ram which he had made, to be brought thither, and to be set against the wall, and to make frequent batteries against it, which with some difficulty, broke down a part of the wall and quite overthrew it.

As we mentioned in our account of the finds in the western casemate chambers, we discovered hundreds of white stone catapult missiles the size of grapefruit. This probably again confirms the report of Josephus, although, as opposed to the siege of Jerusalem and other places which he witnessed, Josephus was not present at the siege of Masada. This probably explains why his description of this event is brief and dry, and does not cover in the same detail how the catapults and the battering ram worked and what counter-action was taken by the defenders. As an illustration of this point, it is worth reading his report of what happened at the siege of Jerusalem:

> The engines, that all the legions had ready prepared for them, were admirably contrived; but still more extraordinary ones belonged to the 'Tenth Legion'; those that threw darts and those that threw stones, were more forcible and larger than the rest; by which they not only repelled the excursions of the Jews, but drove those away that were upon the walls also. Now, the stones that were cast, were of the weight of a talent [half a hundredweight] and were carried two furlongs [about 1,200 feet] and farther. The blow they gave was no way to be sustained, not only by those that stood first in the way, but by those that were beyond them for a great space. As for the Jews, they at first watched the coming of the stone, for it was of a white colour, and could therefore not only be perceived by the great noise it made, but could be seen also before it came, by its brightness; accordingly, the watchmen that sat upon the towers gave them notice when the engine was let go, and the stone came from it and cried out aloud, in their own country language: 'The stone cometh!' so those that were in its way stood off, and threw themselves down upon the ground; by which means, and by their thus guarding themselves, the stone fell down and did them no harm. But the Romans contrived how to prevent that, by blacking the stones, who then could aim at them with success, when the stone was not discerned beforehand, as it had been till then, and so they destroyed many of them at one blow . . .

Josephus is perhaps exaggerating when he records the weight of the stone missiles, but the other details are probably also true of the action at Masada.

What were the defenders on the summit doing while the assault embankment was being laid? They must certainly have tried to interfere with the construction work in every way they could. But the concentration of the

Roman effort on one point made it impossible for the besieged to exert effective counter-pressure to match the enemy on so narrow a front, particularly when the Roman army was able to provide its men with efficient covering fire from its archers – as it did in the action in Jerusalem. And so, as we found in our excavation of several strategic sectors of the summit, the Zealots did not bring their heavy 'rolling' stones into operation since these sectors were not attacked. It may be assumed, however, that a number of such 'rolling' stones *were* used in the western sector against the men building the assault ramp, but to no lasting avail; and in the end, the Romans succeeded in completing it, bringing up their siege engines and making a breach in the casemate wall.

This breach was the work of the battering ram, which was operated from inside the siege-tower, and it was effected directly above the assault embankment. To this day, as our excavation showed, the section of the wall at this spot is missing. Immediately after this action, the defenders sought to seal the breach. This apparently greatly surprised the Romans, as is evident from the words of Josephus who gives a most accurate and detailed account of how it was done:

Breach in casemate wall promptly sealed by defenders

However the Sicarii made haste, and presently built another wall within that, which should not be liable to the same misfortune from the machines with the other; it was made soft and yielding and so was capable of avoiding the terrible blows that affected the other. It was framed after the following manner: they laid together great beams of wood lengthways, one close to the end of another, and the same way in which they were cut. There were two of these rams parallel to one another, and laid at such a distance from each other as the breadth of the wall required, and earth was put into the space between those rams. Now, that the earth might not fall away upon the elevation of this bank to a greater height, they further laid other beams together that lay lengthways. This work of theirs was applied, the blows were weakened by its yieldings; and as the materials by such concussion were shaken closer together, the pile by that means became firmer than before. When Silva saw this, he thought it best to endeavour the taking of this wall by setting fire to it; so he gave orders that the soldiers should throw a great number of burning torches upon it. Accordingly, as it was chiefly made of wood, it soon took fire; and when it was once set on fire, its hollowness made that fire spread to a mighty flame.

There now occurred that very event which we touched upon at the beginning of the book when describing the climatic conditions at Masada and the unpredictable winds. Here is the account by Josephus:

Now, at the very beginning of this fire, a north wind that then blew proved terrible to the Romans; for by bringing the flame downwards, it drove it upon them, and they were almost in despair of success, as fearing their machines would be burnt; but after this, on a sudden the wind changed into the south, as if it were done by divine providence and blew strongly and drove it against the wall, which was now on fire through its entire thickness. So the Romans, having now assistance from God returned to their camp with joy, and resolved to attack their enemies the very next day; on which occasion they set their watch more carefully that night, lest any of the Jews should run away from them without being discovered.

18 The dramatic end

It was then that the tragic drama was enacted on the summit of Masada. It seems appropriate to include here the detailed description of that dramatic event in the words of Josephus:

Josephus' account of the Roman conquest of Masada

'However, neither did Eleazar once think of flying away, nor would he permit any one else to do so; but when he saw their wall burnt down by the fire, and could devise no other way of escaping, or room for their further courage, and setting before their eyes what the Romans would do to them, their children, and their wives, if they got them into their power, he consulted about having them all slain. Now, as he judged this to be the best thing they could do in their present circumstances, he gathered the most courageous of his companions together, and encouraged them to take that course by a speech he made to them in the manner following: "Since we, long ago, my generous friends, resolved never to be servants to the Romans, nor to any other than to God himself, who alone is the true and just Lord of mankind, the time is now come that obliges us to make that resolution true in practice. And let us not at this time bring a reproach upon ourselves for self-contradiction, while we formerly would not undergo slavery, though it were then without danger, but must now, together with slavery, choose such punishments also as are intolerable; I mean this, upon the supposition that the Romans once reduce us under their power while we are alive. We were the very first that revolted from them, and we are the last that fight against them; and I cannot but esteem it as a favour that God hath granted us, that it is still in our power to die bravely, and in a state of freedom, which hath not been the case with others who were conquered unexpectedly. It is very plain that we shall be taken within a day's time; but it is still an eligible thing to die after a glorious manner, together with our dearest friends. This is what our enemies themselves cannot by any means hinder, although they be very desirous to take us alive. Nor can we propose to ourselves any more to fight them and beat them. It had been proper indeed for us to have conjectured at the purpose of God much sooner, and at the very first, when we were so desirous of defending our liberty, and when we received such sore treatment from one another, and worse treatment from our enemies, and to have been sensible that the same God, who had of old taken the Jewish nation into his favour, had now condemned them to destruction; for had he either continued favourable, or been but in a lesser degree displeased with us, he had not overlooked the destruction of so many men, or delivered his most holy city to be burnt and demolished by our enemies. To be sure, we weakly hoped to have preserved ourselves, and ourselves alone, still in a state of freedom, as we had been guilty of no sins ourselves against God, nor been partners with those of others; we also taught other men to preserve their liberty. Wherefore, consider how God hath convinced us that our hopes were in vain, by bringing such distress upon us in the desperate state we are now in, and which is beyond all our expectations; for the nature of this fortress, which was in itself unconquerable, hath not proved a means of our deliverance; and even while we have still great abundance of food, and a great quantity of arms and other necessaries more than we want, we are openly deprived by God himself of all hope of deliverance; for that fire which was driven upon our enemies did not, of its own accord, turn back upon the wall which we had built: this was the effect of God's anger against us for our manifold sins, which we have been guilty of in a most insolent and extravagant manner with regard to our own countrymen; the punishments of which let us not receive from the Romans, but from God himself, as executed by our own hands, for these will be more moderate than the other. Let our wives die before they are abused, and our children before they have tasted of slavery; and after we have slain them, let us bestow that glorious benefit upon one another mutually, and preserve ourselves in freedom, as an excellent funeral monument for us. But first let us destroy our money and the fortress by fire; for I am well assured that this will be a great grief to the Romans, that they shall not be able to seize upon our bodies, and shall fail of our wealth also: and let us spare nothing but our provisions; for they will be a testimonial when we are dead that we were not subdued for want of necessaries; but that, according to our original resolution, we have preferred death before slavery."

Eleazar's plan for the end of the Zealots

'This was Eleazar's speech to them. Yet did not the opinions of all the soldiers acquiesce therein; but although some of them were very zealous to put his advice in practice, and were in a manner filled with pleasure at it, and thought death to be a good thing, yet had those that were most effeminate a commiseration for their wives and families; and when these men were especially moved by the prospect of their own certain death, they looked wistfully at one another, and by the tears that were in their eyes, declared their dissent from his opinion. When Eleazar saw these people in such fear, and that their souls were dejected at so prodigious a proposal, he was afraid lest perhaps these effeminate persons should, by their lamentations and tears, enfeeble those that heard what he had said courageously; so he did not leave off exhorting them, but stirred up himself, and recollecting proper arguments for raising their courage, he undertook to speak more briskly and fully to them, and that concerning the immortality of the soul. So he made a lamentable groan, and fixing his eyes intently on those that wept, he spake thus: "Truly, I was greatly mistaken when I thought to be assisting to brave men who struggled hard for their liberty, and to such as were resolved either to live with honour, or else to die; but I find that you are such people as are no better than others, either in virtue or in courage, and are afraid of dying.

' ". . . Are not we, therefore, ashamed to have lower notions than the Indians? and by our own cowardice to lay a base reproach upon the laws of our country, which are so much desired and imitated by all mankind? But put the case that we had been brought up under another persuasion, and taught that life is the greatest good which men are capable of, and that death is a calamity: however, the circumstances we are now in, ought to be an inducement to us to bear such calamity courageously, since it is by the will of God, and by necessity, that we are to die: for it now appears that God hath made such a decree against the whole Jewish nation, that we are to be deprived of this life which (he knew) we would not make a due use of; for do not you ascribe the occasion of your present condition to yourselves, nor think the Romans are the true occasion that this war we have had with them is become so destructive to us all: these things have not come to pass by their power, but a more powerful cause hath intervened, and made us afford them an occasion of their appearing to be conquerors over us. What Roman weapons, I pray you, were those, by which the Jews of Caesarea were slain? On the contrary, when they were no way disposed to rebel, but were all the while keeping their seventh day festival, and did not so much as lift up their hands against the citizens of Caesarea, yet did those citizens run upon them in great crowds, and cut their throats, and the throats of their wives and children, and this without any regard to the Romans themselves, who never took us for their enemies, till we revolted from them. But some may be ready to say, that truly the people of Caesarea had always a quarrel against those that lived among them, and that when an opportunity offered itself, they only satisfied the old rancour they had against them. What then shall we say to those of Scythopolis, who ventured to wage war with us on account of the Greeks? Nor did they do it by way of revenge upon the Romans, when they acted in concert with our countrymen. Wherefore you see how little our good-will and fidelity to them that profited us, while they were slain, they and their whole families after the most inhuman manner; which was all the requital that was made them for the assistance they had afforded to the others; for that very same destruction which they had prevented from falling upon the others, did they suffer themselves from them, as if they had been ready to be the actors against them. It would be too long for me to speak at this time of every destruction brought upon us: for you cannot but know, that there was not any one Syrian city which did not slay their Jewish inhabitants and were not more bitter enemies to us than were the Romans themselves: nay, even those of Damascus, when they were able to allege no tolerable pretence against us, filled their city with the most barbarous slaughter of our people, and cut the throats of 18,000 Jews, with their wives and children. And as to the multitude of those that were slain in Egypt, and that with torments also, we have been informed there were more than 60,000; those indeed being in a foreign country, and so naturally meeting with nothing to oppose against their enemies, were killed in the manner forementioned. As for all those of us who have waged war against the Romans in our country, had we not sufficient reason to have sure hopes of victory? For we had arms, and walls, and fortresses so prepared as not to be easily taken, and courage not to be moved by any dangers in the cause of liberty, which encouraged us all to revolt from the Romans. But then, these advantages sufficed us but for a short time, and only raised our hopes, while they really appeared to be the origin of our miseries; for all we had, hath been taken from us, and all hath fallen under our enemies, as if these advantages were only to render their victory over us the more glorious, and were not disposed for the preservation of those by whom these preparations were made. And as for those that were already dead in the war, it is reasonable we should esteem them blessed, for they are dead in defending, and not in betraying their liberty; but as to the multitude of those that are now under the Romans, who would not pity their condition? And who would not make haste to die, before he would suffer the same miseries with them? Some of them have been put upon the rack, and tortured with fire and whippings, and so died. Some have been half-devoured by wild beasts, and yet have been preserved alive to be devoured by them a second time, in order to afford laughter and sport to our enemies; and such of those as are alive still, are to be looked on as the most miserable, who, being so desirous of death, could not come at it. And where is now that great city, the metropolis of the Jewish nation, which was fortified by so many walls round about, which had so many fortresses and large towers to defend it, which could hardly contain the instruments prepared for the war, and which had so many ten thousands of men to fight for it? Where is this city that was believed to have God himself inhabiting therein? It is now demolished to the very foundations; and hath nothing but that monument of it preserved, I mean the camp of those that have destroyed it, which still dwells upon its ruins; some unfortunate old men also lie upon the ashes of the temple, and a few women are there preserved alive by the enemy, for our bitter shame and reproach. Now, who is there that revolves these things in his mind, and yet is able to bear the sight of the sun, though he might live out of danger? Who is there so much his country's enemy, or so unmanly, and so desirous of living, as not to repent that he is still alive? And I cannot but wish that we had all died before we had seen that holy city demolished by the hands of our enemies, or the foundations of our holy temple dug up after so profane a manner. But since we had a generous hope that deluded us, as if we might perhaps have been able to avenge ourselves on our enemies on that account, though it be now become vanity, and hath left us alone in this distress, let us make haste to die bravely. Let us pity ourselves, our children, and our wives, while it is in our power to shew pity to them; for we are born to die, as well as those were whom we have begotten; nor is it in the power of the most happy of our race to avoid it. But for abuses and slavery, and the sight of our wives led away after an ignominious manner, with their children, these are not such evils as are natural and necessary

Death preferable to miseries of slavery

among men; although such as do not prefer death before those miseries, when it is in their power so to do, must undergo even them, on account of their own cowardice. We revolted from the Romans with great pretensions to courage; and when at the very last they invited us to preserve ourselves, we would not comply with them. Who will not, therefore, believe that they will certainly be in a rage at us, in case they can take us alive? Miserable will then be the young men, who will be strong enough in their bodies to sustain many torments! Miserable also will be those of elder years, who will not be able to bear those calamities which young men might sustain! One man will be obliged to hear the voice of his son imploring help of his father, when his hands are bound: but certainly our hands are still at liberty, and have a sword in them: let them then be subservient to us in our glorious design; let us die before we become slaves under our enemies, and let us go out of the world, together with our children and our wives, in a state of freedom. This it is that our laws command us to do; this it is that our wives and children crave at our hands; nay, God himself hath brought this necessity upon us; while the Romans desire the contrary, and are afraid lest any man should die before we are taken. Let us therefore make haste, and instead of affording them so much pleasure, as they hope for in getting us under their power, let us leave them an example which shall at once cause their astonishment at our death, and their admiration of our hardiness therein."

'Now as Eleazar was proceeding on in this exhortation, they all cut him off short, and made haste to do the work, as full of an unconquerable ardour of mind, and moved with a demoniacal fury. So they went their ways, as one still endeavouring to be before another, and as thinking that this eagerness would be a demonstration of their courage and good conduct, if they could avoid appearing in the last class: so great was the zeal they were in to slay their wives and children, and themselves also! Nor indeed, when they came to the work itself, did their courage fail them as one might imagine it would have done; but they then held fast the same resolution, without wavering, which they had upon the hearing of Eleazar's speech, while yet every one of them still retained the natural passion of love to themselves and their families, because the reasoning they went upon, appeared to them to be very just, even with regard to those that were *Each man* dearest to them; for the husbands tenderly embraced their wives and took *despatched his own* their children into their arms, and gave the longest parting kisses to them, *family* with tears in their eyes. Yet at the same time did they complete what they had resolved on, as if they had been executed by the hands of strangers, and they had nothing else for their comfort but the necessity they were in of doing this execution, to avoid that prospect they had of the miseries they were to suffer from their enemies. Nor was there at length any one of these men found that scrupled to act their part in this terrible execution, but every one of them despatched his dearest relations. Miserable men indeed were they! whose distress forced them to slay their own wives and children with their own hands, as the lightest of those evils that were before them.

So they not being able to bear the grief they were under for what they had done, any longer, and esteeming it an injury to those they had slain, to live even the shortest space of time after them – they presently laid all they had in a heap, and set fire to it. They then chose ten men by lot out of them, to slay all the rest; every one of whom laid himself down by his wife and children on the ground, and threw his arms about them, and they offered their necks to the stroke of those who by lot executed that melancholy office; and when these ten had, without fear, slain them all, they made the same rule for casting lots for themselves, that he whose lot it was should first kill the other nine, and after all, should kill himself. Accordingly, all those had courage sufficient to be no way behind one another, in doing or suffering; so, for a conclusion, the nine offered their necks to the executioner, and he who was the last of all, took a view of all the other bodies, lest perchance some or other among so many that were slain should want his assistance to be quite despatched; and when he perceived that they were all slain, he set fire to the palace, and with the great force of his hand ran his sword entirely through himself, and fell down dead near to his own relations. So these people died with this intention, that they would not have so much as one soul among them all alive to be subject to the Romans. Yet was there an ancient woman, and another who was of kin to Eleazar, and superior to most women in prudence and learning, with five children, who had concealed themselves in caverns underground, and had carried water thither for their drink, and were hidden there when the rest were intent upon the slaughter of one another. These others were 960 in number, the women and children being withal included in that computation. This calamitous slaughter was made on the fifteenth day of the month (Xanthicus) Nisan.

'Now for the Romans, they expected that they should be fought in the morning, when accordingly they put on their armour, and laid bridges of planks upon their ladders from their banks, to make an assault upon the fortress, which they did; but saw nobody as an enemy, but a terrible solitude on every side, with a fire within the place, as well as a perfect silence. So they were at a loss to guess at what had happened. At length they made a shout, as if it had been at a blow given by a battering-ram, to try whether they could bring any one out that was within; the women heard this noise and came out of their underground cavern, and informed the Romans what had been done, as it was done; and the second of them clearly described all both what was said and what was done, and the manner of it; yet did they not easily give their attention to such a desperate undertaking, and did not believe it could be as they said; they also attempted to put the fire out, and quickly cutting themselves a way through it, they came within the palace, and so met with the multitude of the slain, but could take no pleasure in the fact, though it were done to their enemies. Nor could they do other than wonder at the courage of their resolution, and at the immovable contempt of death which so great a number of them had shown, when they went through with such an action as that was.'

Ten men chosen by lots to kill the rest

The last remaining man set fire to the palace

Only two women and five children escaped by hiding

Wonder of Romans at such an action

The three terraces of the palace-villa and the Roman ramp are clear in
this engraving by Tipping of the north-west cliff of Masada.

19 The pioneers

Masada is now more widely known than it ever was, even in its Herodian heyday. With access to it made easy and safe it is destined to cast its spell over countless visitors in the years to come. But it has taken 125 years to unlock its secrets, beginning when two travellers, looking from a distance at the rock which Arabs called es-Sebbeh, first identified it as the historical Masada, and ending with an international army passing its ancient dust through their fingers.

The two travellers were the American scholar, Edward Robinson and his companion E. Smith. Robinson himself did not visit Masada, but after visiting Ein Gedi in 1838, he wrote:

First travellers to Masada

> My attention was particularly directed to the ruin called by the Arabs Sebbeh, already mentioned as situated towards the south upon a pyramidal cliff rising precipitously from the sea, just beyond Wadi es-Seyal. The truncated summit of the lofty isolated rock forms a small plain apparently inaccessible; and this is occupied by the ruin. We had been greatly struck by its appearance and on examining it closely with a telescope, I could perceive what appeared to be a building on its N.W. part and also traces of other buildings further east ... Subsequent research leaves little room to doubt that this was the site of the ancient and renowned fortress of Masada ...

In a footnote Robinson adds:

> The first suggestion as to the identity of Sebbeh with Masada, I owe to my companion, Mr Smith ...

The credit for this identification should, thus, go to E. Smith.

In addition, Robinson correctly identified Herod's palace – a suggestion which was not followed up by later scholars:

> The building now visible on the N.W. and the columns described by the Arabs are not improbably the remains of Herod's Palace.

Further he remarked:

> ... there is little doubt that future travellers who may visit its site, will find other and more definite traces of its ancient strength.

This last remark prompted the American missionary, S.W. Wolcott and the English painter Tipping, to visit Masada and even to draw it.

Wolcott's words in this connection – the first since Josephus' description – are well worth quoting, as are the drawings by W. Tipping which are reproduced:

Wolcott's
description

The rock of Sebbeh is opposite to the peninsula, and is itself separated from the water's edge by a shoal or sand-bank, two or three miles in width, from north to south. This extends out, on the northern side of the cliff, which projects beyond the mountain range. The mountains on the south are in a line with it, and of the same height, and it is separated from them by the deep and precipitous Wadi Sinein. On the west, a smaller wadi separates it from more moderate hills, above which it rises. Its insulation is thus complete. We encamped at the western base; and after resting a little made the ascent from the same side, and accomplished it without difficulty, using occasionally both hands and feet, and proceeding at the steepest point on an embankment which remains. This is the only spot where the rock can now be climbed; the pass on the east, described by Josephus, seems to have been swept away. The language of that historian respecting the loftiness of the site is not very extravagant. It requires firm nerves to stand upon the verge of its steepest sides, and look directly down. The depth at these points cannot be less than a thousand feet, and we thought it more. The highest points of the rock are on the north, and the south-west; the ground sloping in a gentle wadi towards the south-east corner. The whole area we estimated at three quarters of a mile in length, from north to south, and a third of a mile in breadth. There are no traces of vegetation, except in the bottoms of some of the open cisterns. On approaching the rock from the west, the 'white promontory', as Josephus appropriately calls it, is seen on this side near the northern end. This is the point where the siege was pressed and carried; and here we ascended. Both before and after the ascent we observed the 'wall built round about the entire top of the hill by King Herod'; all the lower part of which remains. Its colour was the same dark red as the rock, though it is said to have been 'composed of white stone'; but on breaking the stone, it appeared that it was naturally whitish, and had been burnt brown by the sun.

In the existing foundations we could trace only the general outlines of the structures which Josephus describes. The peculiar form of some, composed of long parallel rooms, indicated that they had been storehouses or barracks, rather than private dwellings. The architecture, both of the wall and of the buildings, was of one kind, consisting of rough stones quarried probably on the summit, laid loosely together, and the interstices filled in with small pieces of stone. It had the appearance of cobbled work. We thought, at first, it could hardly be the work of Herod; but there can be no doubt that it is so. The stone is of the most durable kind, and there are no traces of more ancient work; and these would be almost the only materials accessible in such a spot. Near the head of the ascent is a modern ruin, consisting chiefly of a gate-way of square hewn stones, with a pointed arch. We saw no other architecture which we thought to be of the same age. Near this is a small building with a circular recess in the eastern wall of its principal room. Forty or fifty feet below the northern summit, are the foundations of a round tower, to which we did not attempt to descend. Nearby are windows cut in the rock, with their sides whitened, probably belonging to some large cistern now covered up. We found a cistern excavated in the south-west corner of the rock, with similar windows in its southern end at the top, and with a descent to a doorway in the top of its northern end, from which a flight of steps descends into the cistern itself. It is nearly fifty feet deep, a hundred long, and forty broad; and its walls are still

Tipping's engraving of the southern end of Masada. The figures stand
near Roman camp H; Roman camp G is drawn above them.

covered with a white cement, which served us for an album. The other cisterns that
we saw were not large; and some of them were still covered over with small round
arches. Fragments of pottery lay scattered on the surface of the rock; but the relic
which perhaps interested us the most, was without the rock, on the ground below.
Josephus says, that the Roman general 'built a wall quite around the entire
fortress'. As we stood on the summit of the rock, we could trace every part of that
wall, carried along the low ground, and, wherever it met a precipice, commencing
again on the high summit above; thus making the entire circuit of the place. Connected with it, at intervals, were the walls of the Roman camps, built as described
by Josephus in his chapter on the Roman armies and camps. The principal camps
were opposite the north-west and south-east corners; the former being the spot
where Josephus places that of the Roman general. The outline of the works, as seen
from the heights above, is as complete as if they had been but recently abandoned.
We afterwards examined the wall in places; and found it six feet broad, and built
like the walls above but more rudely; it had of course crumbled, and was probably
never high. It brought the siege before us with an air of reality; and recalled to our

minds, as we looked upon it, the awful immolation which had taken place on the spot where we stood. It was also a stupendous illustration of the Roman perseverance, that subdued the world, which could sit down so deliberately, in such a desert, and commence a siege with such a work; and, I may add, which could scale such a fortress. We found among the rocks below a round stone, which had probably been hurled from a catapult. We launched, by way of diversion, some of the large stones from the original wall towards the Dead Sea; none of which reached the Roman lines, half a mile or more distant; though some of them stopped not far short, making the most stupendous bounds. I was desirous of making the circuit of the rock. The declivity which we had descended in reaching it left us on an offset of the mountains, still several hundred feet above the sea. The wadi which runs on the west of the cliff, is on this elevation. But at the extremities of the rock, the ground suddenly breaks down into deep fissures, and soon reached the lower level. I followed the above wadi southwards; and found that the cleft which forms the southern boundary of the rock, was a perpendicular descent from it. The south-west corner of the rock, forms a kind of bastion, opposite to which the side of the wadi is shelving. Descending here carefully, I reached the bottom, walled in on three sides, by rocky ramparts, their sombre craggy peaks frowning above, while torn and disjointed masses from them strewed the bed of the valley. I followed this chasm descending steeply east by north, and in an hour from leaving the tent had not reached the east side of the rock; when I was arrested by the shouts of our Arabs on the cliff behind me, calling and beckoning to me to return. The reason I soon discovered in the appearance of three wild Bedawin with clubs, whom they had noticed, who accosted me with a demand for a bakhshish; which however they showed no disposition to enforce. This of course put an end to further observations in that quarter – fortunately, perhaps, as in any event the circuit would have been longer and more fatiguing than I had contemplated. It was one of the most interesting circumstances connected with Sebbeh, that it commanded a complete view of the Dead Sea, which lay beneath us in its length and breadth. We spread the map before us; and were struck with its general accuracy. The peninsula appears to the eye as a flat sand-bank, in striking contrast with the bold mountains which tower above it. Though furrowed by the waters it is still a plain. We remained at Sebbeh until March 15th; our Arabs having been kept contented the last day by a feast upon a Beden, shot on the top of the rock. Our own supplies were getting low. We had been informed that there was water near; but could obtain it only from the collections which the recent rains had left in the hollows of the rocks; confirming the remark of Josephus, that water as well as food was brought hither to the Roman army from a distance.

This remarkable spot, therefore, as thus described and delineated, may now with advantage be thought of as bearing out those statements and those descriptions of Masada which we find in *The Jewish War*. Confidently it may be affirmed that in few instances where topographical identity is in question, have modern researches better sustained the testimony of an ancient writer than they do in this instance. It is manifest that Josephus must personally, and at leisure, have made himself acquainted with this spot: he had visited it – whether previously to the fall of his country, or afterwards; and in this case, as in others which have come before us, he proves himself to have been conversant with the facts he has to do with – observant of details, and quite as trustworthy in his reports of them as ancient writers generally are.

Josephus was not familiar, as modern travellers are, with the vastness of Alpine scenery, and therefore he was not prepared to use measured terms in speaking of heights and depths, such as those of Palestine. Those who, on their way to Palestine, sojourn in Switzerland, have already spent their stock of wonder, and have quite exhausted their stores of hyperbolic phrases. But Josephus, when he speaks of chasms on either hand, that inspire terror in the boldest minds, and of 'depths which the eye cannot measure', speaks as one does who has been conversant only with the precipices of a thousand or of twelve hundred feet; nor is it equitable when he does so, to accuse him of indulging a habit of culpable exaggeration. Masada and its remains must be allowed to corroborate, in a very remarkable manner, the averments of the author of the *Wars of the Jews*.

Wolcott and Tipping indeed identified correctly a number of important objects at Masada (though not all were accepted by later scholars) and among these were the 'leuce' (the white promontory), the wall surrounding the top of Masada and the stores. They also spotted the 'round tower' and its adjacent 'pools', the large pool and the Roman circumvallation and camps. Moreover, they even fixed correctly Silva's H Q in camp F. They also recognised the accuracy of Josephus' descriptions. Indeed, it is amazing how accurate were the impressions of those first pioneers, of some of the most important objects on Masada.

Of the descriptions of the many explorers and expeditions who followed Wolcott, I would like to quote mainly those who have enriched our knowledge. The first was the expedition of the American naval officer J. W. Lynch, who explored the Dead Sea in his boats. On 29 April 1848 he despatched a number of his assistants to visit Masada, while he himself remained in his camp, and then: *Other explorers' descriptions*

... at noon, fired out at sea, in honour of the illustrious dead, twenty one-minute guns from the heavy blunderbuss mounted on the bow of the *Fanny Mason*.

Towards evening his men returned from Masada and reported details which he records in his book. Although they wrongly took the 'Roman Ascent' north of Masada for the 'snake path', they were the first to assume that the 'holes' on the north-western precipice – which they had been unable to reach – were water reservoirs. They also spotted the 'square building':

... forty or fifty feet below that, on another ledge the foundation walls of a square enclosure, with a triangular wall abutting with the angles of its base upon the walls of the circular tower, and the west side of the square enclosure. They found it impossible to descend to examine these ruins.

Like Wolcott and Tipping, Lynch's officers, too, seem to have enjoyed rolling stones from the cliff:

The officers amused themselves by displacing some of the stones and sending them over the cliff, and watching them as they whirled and bounded to the base, upwards of 1200 feet down, with more fearful velocity than the stones from the Roman ballistae when Silva pressed the siege.

Even with the volunteers of our expedition, stone-rolling and watching the stones hit the bottom and smash to bits was a popular pastime.

In January 1851, the French scholar, F. de Saulcy, visited Masada, and he, too, wrongly identified the 'snake path' in the north. He climbed up via the Roman ramp, which he identified correctly, but erroneously attributed the Byzantine gate to Herod. Even though he made the relatively easy western climb, he exclaimed with relief on reaching the top: 'Thank Heaven! We have reached it with sound limbs!'

De Saulcy – as already mentioned when describing the chapel – did some digging in the structure which he considered a palace, in order to discover its mosaics, and here is his report:

> Some small detached cubes of red, white and black stone induce me to suppose that the hall is paved with real mosaic; I therefore tempt my Bedouins with the promise of a bakhshish and whilst I am drawing the plans of the different apartments, and Belly is engaged in making a sketch of this extraordinary ruin, the rubbish is cleaned from the floor, and a handsome mosaic pavement, disposed in circular knots, is brought once more to light. Unfortunately all is broken in pieces; I feel therefore, no scruple in carrying away some specimens.

It is not clear how many specimens de Saulcy did carry away, but the fact is that very little remained of the floor. He considered the stores to be structures of the period of Jonathan, and it is strange that he identified the large pool as a storehouse! Considering that he only stayed two hours on top of Masada, he managed a great deal and it is to him that we owe the first published plan – though quite inaccurate – of Masada and the siege camps.

In 1852, the Dutch scholar and naval officer Van de Velde visited

Fragment of the mosaic floor in the main hall of the chapel.

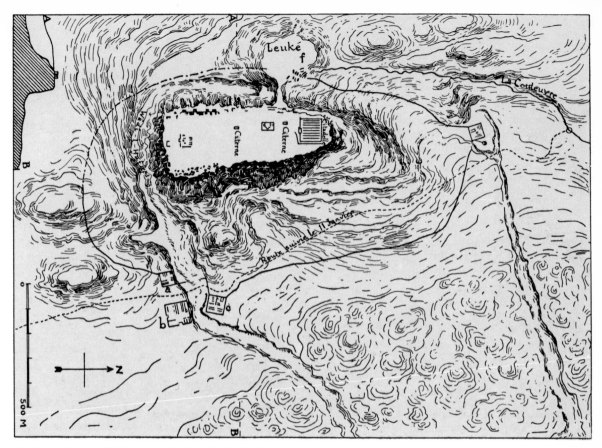

De Saulcy's plan of Masada – the first plan to be drawn.

Masada and in 1854 published his impressions. Though not much new information was revealed by him, he was the very first to recognise the chapel for what it was.

The next name worthy of mention is that of the scholar E. Guillaume Rey, who came to Masada on 24 January 1858. He published a plan more detailed than the one by de Saulcy, but made a number of gross mistakes when identifying buildings. He rejected de Saulcy's suggestion of identifying the chapel as a palace, offering instead his theory that it was a bath-house of Herod's period, and considered the stores were barracks. On the other hand it is interesting to note that he correctly identified the upper terrace – on which he found remains of a mosaic floor – with Herod's palace as described by Josephus. He discarded de Saulcy's opinion that the Byzantine gate was Herodian, and attributed it instead to the Arab period. He, too, mistook the large pool for stores.

In 1863, the German scholar F. Tuch published a book on Masada in the light of Josephus' descriptions and those of travellers up to his time. Although he himself did not visit Masada, his book is a turning-point in the analysis of the sources of Masada's history.

245

This aerial view of the storerooms at the beginning of the excavations explains
how the parallel walls seemed to Tristram like lines of defence.

H. B. Tristram visited Masada in 1864 and again in 1871, and in his books *Land of Israel* and *Land of Moab* described his impressions of Masada. Tristram, ascending from the west, must have found the descriptions of earlier scholars about the difficult ascent rather exaggerated, since he says: 'An English lady could accomplish it easily . . .' Tristram measured the height of the cliff and erroneously came up with 2,200 feet above Dead Sea level:

We measured the height of the peak barometrically, and found it exactly 2,200 feet from the level of the Dead Sea.

He tried unsuccessfully to descend to the 'Round Tower' and the 'square structure' but could only record his amazement at these ' fortifications':

It was difficult to conceive for what strategic purpose these ramparts could have been occupied, at such enormous cost of labour, since they must have been wholly untenable when the city was captured.

Had he read Josephus, and even Robinson, more carefully, he might have arrived at the true answer; this privilege thus fell to Israeli youngsters almost a hundred years later.

Interestingly enough Tristram, too, realised the marvellous acoustic conditions between the cliff and the base which we mentioned when speaking of the Roman siege:

As I sat astride a projecting rock on the north peak, I could look down from giddy heights, 1,500 feet, on both sides and in front; and yet so clear was the atmosphere, and so extraordinary its power of conveying sound, that I could carry on conversation with my friends in the camp below, and compare barometers and observations.

It is astonishing how an otherwise sound scholar like Tristram remained helpless vis-à-vis archaeological data. Although the storehouses with their parallel walls had already been described by his predecessors, he writes of them as follows:

. . . from this wall, at right angles, run twenty-one parallel walls, or heaps of rough masonry, for the most part thrown down into ridges . . . what this extraordinary accumulation of masonry may have been, unless constructed as a breastwork for the last desperate defence foot by foot, I do not presume to conjecture.

He identified the chapel as such during his first visit, but attributed it to the Middle Ages. On his second visit he changed his mind and said it was a synagogue. However, the surrounding landscape must have attracted him no less than the actual ruins, and we can easily agree with his description:

Looking down from the top, the whole of the Dead Sea spread out as in a map . . . It was a picture of stern grandeur and desolate magnificence, perhaps unequalled in the world.

Tristram's plan of Masada, however, must have been drawn from memory alone . . .

Overleaf: This aerial view looking towards the south shows the 'snake path' on the left leading to the south of the storehouse complex.

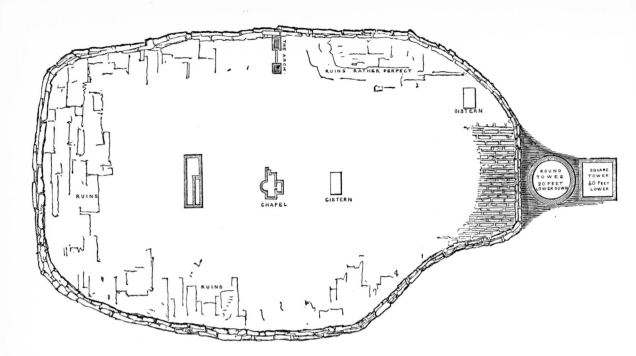

Tristram's plan of Masada. The middle and lower terraces were recorded correctly; all the rest must have been done from memory.

An important turning-point in Masada research came with the 'Survey of Western Palestine', carried out on behalf of the Palestine Exploration Fund (now celebrating its centenary), and headed by Kitchener, Warren and Conder. It is to Warren that we are indebted for the discovery of the location of the 'snake path', or at least part of it. He was the first – in 1867 – to climb Masada from the east. His description of this climb is so vivid, that it is worth quoting in full:

Warren's description   Our men [i.e. the three Bedouin] had never been up before, and as we were on the wrong side we felt doubtful whether we should double the southern side of the fortress and so get into the regular path, or should go towards the north. Circumstances guided us: we found that full on the eastern side we had less difficulty and we thought to creep round at a higher level; when, however, we were about half way up we saw right above us a sort of broken path and we were so knocked up that the danger of the short cut appeared as nothing to the long pull round. We commenced scrambling up by a path more dangerous than difficult, for the natural lay of the rocks is such that they crop out perpendicular to the steep side of the hill, and thus each stone you scramble up is overhanging and ready to topple over and crush you, should your weight be sufficient to overbalance it.

One of the Bedouin suddenly disappeared over a rock; suspecting him, I caught him before he had quite finished the flask of water with which he had been entrusted. On getting close to the top we were nearly stumped; before us were two upright pieces of wall, of about fifteen feet each in height, without any apparent path; we found some toe-holes in these, and climbed up. A false step here would

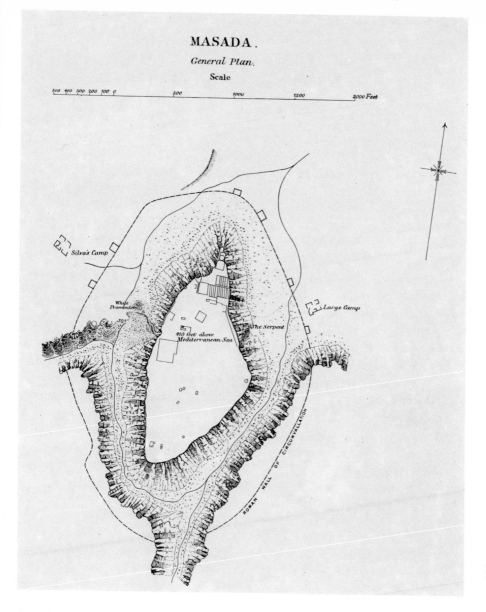

MASADA.

General Plan.

Scale

500 400 300 200 100 0   500   1000   1500   2000 Feet

Silva's Camp

White Promontory

410 feet above Mediterranean Sea

The Serpent

Large Camp

ROMAN WALL OF CIRCUMVALLATION

Conder's plan of Masada and the Roman camps. The position of the 'snake path' is marked by 'the serpent'.

have been destruction: we arrived at the top at 5.20 (having started the climb at 2.20) and gave three cheers, re-echoed from below: we found we had landed full on the middle of the eastern side of the flat surface of the fortress. Whether the path we went up by or came down by is the 'serpent' spoken of by Josephus, appears to be a question which cannot be solved by reference to Whiston's translation; but it seems probable that it should refer to the more difficult path to the east, by which we ascended.

After arguing with the opinions of his predecessors as to the place of the 'snake path', Warren was pleased with his discovery, which 'so far helped in a small way to verify the descriptions of the Jewish historian'.

On the mapping of Masada, the turning-point was brought about by

Conder on behalf of the Survey, when he stayed at Masada one day in March 1875. The weather conditions which he describes remind me vividly of the ones experienced by us:

We executed a traverse survey of the top with the prismatic compass and tape, and special plan of the chapel. We also fixed the positions of the Roman camps below. A very severe gale of wind came on, and we found great difficulty in taking our observations. I was disappointed in the hope of descending to the Tower at the north angle [i.e. the 'middle terrace' of the villa-palace – Y.Y.] being afraid to venture in so strong a wind 70 feet down over the edge of the precipice, although I had brought ladders and ropes for the purpose.

Lieutenant Conder, too, could not help admiring the accuracy of Josephus' descriptions.

The first point which strikes one on approaching the ruin and climbing to the plateau is the wonderful exactitude of the description by Josephus.

His great discovery was the ruins of the large structure on the west (the western palace) and it was he who proposed identifying them (erroneously, as we know today) with Herod's palace described by Josephus. Conder's plans, published by the Survey, were the first to approach reality in some degree as the illustrations show.

A. v. Domaszewski's studies of Masada

The earliest investigation of the Roman camps can be attributed to the famous scholar A. v. Domaszewski, who, in 1909, published, together with his colleague R.E. Brünnow, their studies on Masada in the third volume of their monumental work *Die Provincia Arabia*. V. Domaszewski, whose particular interest lay in the Roman camps, concentrated mainly on the

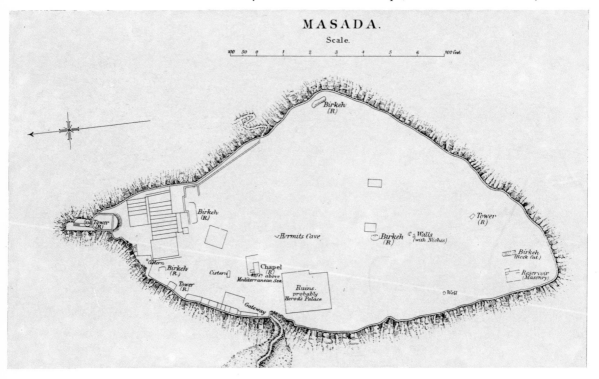

Conder's more detailed plan of Masada; the palace-villa is mostly inaccurate as can be seen by comparison with the expedition's plan.

Praetorium at camp B and camp C. His plan of Masada – based on Rey's with some corrections – is reproduced here.

In 1905 the German scholar G. D. Sandel visited Masada and it is to him that we owe not only the identification of the rows of 'caves' on the north-western cliff as water reservoirs, but also the correct observation that these reservoirs were fed by special canals which drained the rain-water. These discoveries – together with some others already mentioned – seem to have been forgotten with time, and were much later re-discovered by the Israeli youth movements.

The study of the Roman camps advanced greatly after Christopher Hawkes of the British Museum published (in *Antiquity*, 1929) a thorough study based on air photographs taken by the RAF in 1924 and 1928. (I was very touched by a letter from one of the pilots who took these photographs at the time, congratulating me on the excavations at Masada – he had read about them in the London *Observer*.) But even that study was not complete, and as I have already remarked when discussing the Roman camps, it will not be complete before more of the camps are excavated and properly mapped. However, one must mention the thorough studies of Shmaryahu Guttman and Professor Richmond, who have added important details to our knowledge of the subject.

It will not be an overstatement, however, to say that the most profound and pioneering study of the subject was done by the German scholar Adolf Schulten, who was amongst the first scholars to spend a whole month at Masada, in 1932, and it is his plans that laid the foundation for the future study of the ruins. As the head of an expedition who lived at Masada

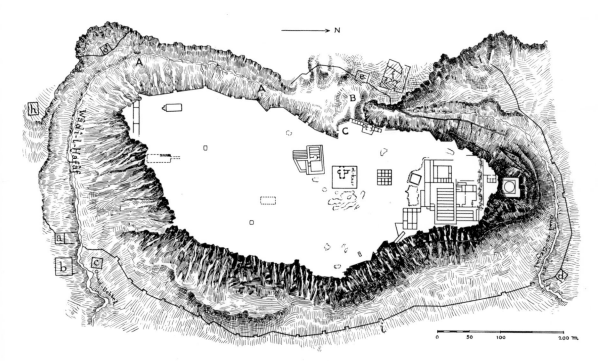

Rey's plan with some corrections by von Domaszewski.

eleven months – longer than Silva – I found Schulten's description of the organisation of his expedition most enlightening. I believe the reader, who has followed our hardships, will also find it of interest:

Schulten's
expedition

We stayed in four tents; two weeks on the eastern side of Masada, near the western wall of camp B, on the edge of the deep Wadi Sebbeh – and two weeks on the western side, on the plateau which served the Romans as a 'building site' [This is where we put up our generators in 1963 – Y.Y.] near the ramp. Our food arrived once a week from Jerusalem, and water – about 70 litres – was brought daily on two donkeys. While we were in the east, the water was carried from Wadi Seyal some ten kilometres away and while in the west, it was brought from Wadi es-Sebbeh nearby. [Rainwater accumulated in rock depressions – Y.Y.] Our meals consisted of rice, tinned meat and vegetables as well as apple-sauce and bread, which dried at once. For drinking we used boiled water and the excellent wine from Sarona, near Jaffa. The Arabs fed on rice, beans, lentils, dried figs and bread. We greatly enjoyed the tasty coffee of the Levant, with which we entertained some of the Bedouins. Our cigarette consumption was enormous and I noticed that the Arabs smoked even more than the Spaniards. We made our way by car up to the mouth of the Jordan, and thence to Masada in Mr Frank's motor-boat. Our way back lasted some 12 hours, partly on foot and partly on donkeys, through the Judean desert to Hebron . . . I consider my stay at Masada the happiest of all my expeditions, though the most exhausting.

I can almost agree with Schulten's words and most certainly with those he wrote at the end of his preface:

One may envy the future explorer of the fort, his task; it is rich and interesting, and the magnificent view alone is ample reward.

In spite of his important contribution to Masada research, Schulten made several fundamental errors. It was he who rejected Robinson's suggestion of identifying the 'hanging palace' described by Josephus with the ruins of the northern cliff. Instead he adopted Conder's suggestion that it was the one in the west, for reasons which were invalid. On the other hand, as we have already seen, both were right in assuming this structure to be a palace. When we began our excavations, we named the western structure 'Schulten's palace' to distinguish it from Herod's palace in the north. But we had to discard this title when we were asked by one visitor if Schulten had been Herod's contemporary or predecessor!

Schulten also completely rejected Warren's discovery of the true location of the 'snake path'; and he thought the structures on the northern cliff were bastions connected with the 'snake path' which he believed came to an end there.

Masada's magic and, in a way, also Schulten's study, prompted the youngsters of the Israeli youth movements to climb to the top and continue the research. To them we owe some corrections of Schulten's errors, and primarily the re-discovery of the 'snake path', the northern palace and the water system. The exact details of the water system and its feeding canals were discovered by Azaria Allon, a member of Kibbutz Beth

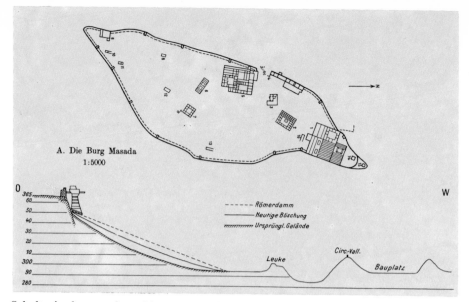

A. Die Burg Masada
1:5000

0

365
60
50
40
30
20
10
300
90
280

W

- - - - - Römerdamm
———— Heutige Böschung
〜〜〜〜〜 Ursprüngl. Gelände

Circ.-Vall.

Leuke

Bauplatz

Schulten's plan together with a cross-section of the Roman ramp.

Hashita; the first publication with plans of the structures on the northern cliff and their identification as the Herodian palace described by Josephus came, in 1953, from the pen of Micha Livneh, member of Kibbutz Ma'ayan Baruch.

There is no doubt, however, that the major role in turning Masada into the educational attraction and place of pilgrimage it has become for Israeli youth was played by Shmaryahu Guttman, of Kibbutz Na'an, who for many years had dedicated much of his energy, time and ingenuity to the study of Masada. Not only was he the first – in 1954 – to describe correctly the 'snake path' with all its serpentine turns, but he was also the first to restore the path, excavate its gate and reconstruct the Roman camp A. In addition, he greatly advanced the study of Herod's water system; and finally, it was he who spurred the scientific institutions in Israel to undertake the excavations at Masada.

Thus in 1955–6, survey expeditions set out on behalf of the Israel Exploration Society, the Hebrew University and the Department of Antiquities, co-ordinated by J. Aviram, the honorary secretary of the Israel Exploration Society. They were headed by Professors N. Avigdad, M. Avi-Yonah, Dr Y. Aharoni and Messrs. I. Dunayevski and S. Guttman. Although these expeditions stayed at Masada twice only, ten days each time, they succeeded in discovering much of the northern palace and thus confirmed some of the earlier suggestions. Moreover, they verified certain facts in connection with the storehouse complex and the western structure. Mr Dunayevski, who later joined our expedition as one of its two architects, even prepared a fresh plan of Masada, also using air-photographs. However, even this plan, though far more accurate than its predecessors, required some important alterations by the time we had terminated our job.

Overleaf: A general airview of Masada from the east at the end of first season of excavations. The 'snake path' and its gate can be picked out in the photograph.

This dramatic air-photo of Masada, taken in the afternoon from the west while the sun was low, shows clearly the irregular topography of the top of Masada.

The Masada Archaeological Expedition

P.O.B. 7041, JERUSALEM, ISRAEL

APPLICATION FORM

Family name .... Given name(s) ....

Present address ....

.... Tel. no. ....

Forwarding address after Masada (if different from above) ....

....

Nationality .... Age .... Male/Female

Profession .... Present occupation ....

Business address ....

Education: elementary / secondary / vocational / university

If you have previously worked on an archaeological dig, state

where .... for how long ....

Priority will be given to applicants with knowledge or experience in any of the following capacities (please underline where relevant):

Masonry (building) — drawing — restoration — nursing — conservation of antiquities — surveying —
plumbing — pottery — electricity — mechanics — secretarial — engineering — architecture — ....

Languages (speaking) ....

Please underline the desired work-period(s) in the list below:

Period 1 — Fri., 27 Nov., 64 — Fri., 11 Dec., 64
Period 2 — " 11 Dec., 64 — " 25 Dec., 64
Period 3 — " 25 Dec., 64 — " 8 Jan., 65
Period 4 — " 8 Jan., 65 — " 22 Jan., 65
Period 5 — " 22 Jan., 65 — " 5 Feb., 65
Period 6 — " 5 Feb., 65 — " 19 Feb., 65
Period 7 — " 19 Feb., 65 — " 5 Mar., 65
Period 8 — " 5 Mar., 65 — " 19 Mar., 65
Period 9 — " 19 Mar., 65 — " 2 Apr., 65

Should the desired period be full-up, please put me down for period .... (from .... to ....)
as an alternative.

My parents' permission is enclosed (for applicants between 17–18).

I undertake to perform all duties assigned to me in the excavation as well as my share of camp duties and to abide absolutely at all times by the expedition's rules of discipline.

I know that the expedition will provide me only with food and lodgings and that all other expenses, including my fare, will be borne by me.

I shall make no claims against the expedition and not hold it responsible in any way in case of damage to myself* or to my property.

I know that photography is forbidden at Masada and shall not bring a camera with me. Moreover, I undertake not to publish anything connected with the excavations in any form whatsoever, not to lecture on the Masada discoveries anywhere and not to communicate any information regarding the excavations to the press, TV, radio or otherwise.

I have carefully read the informative letter received with this application form, & fully understood its contents.

To the best of my knowledge I suffer from no disability or chronic or contagious disease which might interfere with my duties on the expedition or affect the health of other members.

Date .... Signature ....

* All volunteers will be insured by the expedition against accidents occuring in the course of their work on the dig.

20 The volunteers

I doubt whether we could have had the success we achieved, or under-taken so much in the time at our disposal, without the volunteers.

I am under no illusions that all who came were prompted by the same motives that moved those of us who were responsible for the expedition. But I am quite certain that after their Masada experience and their return home, Masada and its archaeological, national and historical significance are as much a part of their consciousness as they are of ours.

The volunteers deserve a book to themselves. Here there is space for only a few words about a random few to illustrate the impact of Masada on such diverse types. There were the aged couple from Haifa, looking like the early Zionist pioneers, who had come to Palestine at the beginning of the century. There were no bounds to their joy at having been accepted, despite their age, and though they looked frail, they sought the most physically exacting jobs. Unlike some others, they did not care whether they discovered any-thing or not. Participation was all – participation in the great Masada venture.

An unforgettable character was the young girl from London who had left her artist's studio to join us at the beginning of the first season. She came for a fortnight and stayed till the end. She returned to London, and at the start of the second season she turned up again – all at her own expense – and again stayed till the end. When I first saw her moving heavy boulders, I suggested that she be transferred to lighter work, but she refused adam-antly. Nor did she respond immediately to my expressions of surprise. Later she told me the reason: only while shifting these heavy stones did she feel that she was engaged in something which no one else had done during the last 2,000 years.

There were three other women who worked with us as volunteers on and off throughout both seasons. One was a Haifa housewife. Another was a *kibbutznik*, who used all her accumulated leave – and mortgaged future leaves – to take part in our dig. None was as hard-working as these two; not even the toughest male could compete with them in industry and per-severance and dedication to the objective – to unravel the secrets of Masada. They dug and scraped and sifted – and managed to unearth more than anyone else. The third woman, a middle-aged nursing sister

Opposite: Application form for volunteers for the second season of excavations. Once accepted, volunteers were issued with a special volunteer card.

from Denmark, also set an example of diligence. After a tiring day's work, she would spend her leisure hours helping the camp doctor in the clinic. The doctors were also volunteers, doing fortnightly stints. The Danish nurse stayed with us for the whole of the first season. I do not exaggerate when I credit these three women and the girl from London with a good part of the Masada excavation.

Volunteers of many different nationalities

We had many volunteers from England. One was a captain in the Royal Navy who decided to spend his annual leave with us. He flew to Lod, came straight to Masada, and on completion of his fortnight he flew right back to his base in Britain without having any time to visit other parts of Israel. He worked well, as one would expect of a British naval officer, and he found this unusual task on such a location fascinating. But he had one unexpected moment which had nothing to do with archaeology. It was a contretemps with the expedition's photographer, Aryeh Volk, one of the veteran archaeological photographers in the country – and one of the best – who had been with me at the Hazor excavations. He is an excellent craftsman, and, like many in his profession, can be temperamental. Those who know him know that when he is on the job he insists on absolute silence. When he is photographing, he can get rattled even by the twitter of a bird. The captain did not know this, and when he came to shoot stills of something that the captain had just discovered, the Englishman chatted to a friend. This nettled Volk and an angry exchange followed. When tempers had abated, the two sat down together to 'make it up'. During the course of their talk, it transpired that before the creation of the State of Israel the captain had served on one of the British vessels that was engaged in hunting *Haganah* ships attempting to bring 'illegal' immigrants into the country. He mentioned one they had caught. It turned out to be the very ship on which the photographer had travelled as an 'illegal' immigrant. The two became good friends.

The reason which prompted two other volunteers from England was very moving. We received a letter from an official in London to say that he would like to come and also bring his sixteen-year-old son. He knew that this was below the acceptance age, but he explained: 'My object in bringing my sixteen-year-old son is partly education, but mainly that he may be shown by example to give of his time and labour without financial reward, for the joy of a worthwhile venture alongside young people from other nations.' Of course we accepted both, and I have no doubt that his Masada stay was a significant educational experience for the boy. Incidentally, he also pulled his weight admirably on the dig.

Professions of volunteers

I do not imagine that any other archaeological expedition has boasted such varied types among its participants. We had drivers, psychologists, pathologists, students, models, social workers, camera-men (as diggers), priests, vagabonds, geologists, teachers, physiotherapists, pharmacists, miners, editors, professors, shepherds, farmers, actors, architects, artists, librarians, radio-technicians, company directors, contractors, sculptors, housewives, gardeners, waiters, butlers, lawyers, travel-agents, factory hands, pilots, accountants, advertisers, doctors, potters, draftsmen, physicists, dentists, tourist guides, bankers, builders, nurses, restorers of antiquities, secretaries, clerks, soldiers, midwives, printers, historians, film directors, chambermaids, violin makers, elephant tamers – and archaeologists.

I remember one occasion, while on a morning round of the locations, when I noticed a pair of delicate hands trying to grapple with a stubborn boulder. The hands belonged to a distinguished London doctor, a Harley Street specialist who had come to us with his daughter for a two weeks' stay. I doubt whether he had spent much time in his life on manual labour, and I urged him to try a lighter job. But he would not hear of it. 'This will either make me or break me,' he said. And great was his delight – and so was ours – when a few days later it fell to him to discover a fragment of a rare and most important scroll.

I have already indicated that not all who came were moved by the same ideal. An excellent illustration of this was provided by a French couple who aroused my interest when I had read their application form. Against 'profession', the man had written 'taxi-driver'; his wife, 'chambermaid'. In general, I rarely sought to apologise to the volunteers for the tough living conditions, for they had been warned in advance. But when I visited the southern casemate wall where this couple were working on the first morning after the arrival of the new group, I thought it only right to say a sad word about our food – for that was certainly an area in which the suffering of a Frenchman would be most keen. 'Please don't apologise, sir,' said the taxi-driver, 'We came here to slim!' And, indeed, they succeeded. But even this plump French couple, who had come to lose weight, left with their hearts conquered by Masada. A letter written immediately on their return to France begged me to let them know if and when there would be another season of digging, for all they wished to do was to come back and take further part in the excavations.

It is perhaps fitting to mention one more volunteer – a South-African – who was with us during all the first season, was soon put in charge of all volunteers, and became their 'ambassador' to the 'staff court'. Later he married an American volunteer, and both have now settled near Masada – he to become curator of the site and she to work as a guide.

As for the volunteers from among Israeli youth, they of course knew all about Masada. They knew its dramatic history, and it had long been a challenging objective of youth-group hikes. Now all wished to share in the dig, and those who were accepted were extraordinarily industrious. Seeing them at work scraping walls and clearing floors, I often wished that their parents could see them, for it was doubtful whether they displayed such dedication over chores at home. And how satisfying it was that it should be they, the young generation of newly-independent Israel, who should uncover the heart-rending remains of the last Jewish defenders of Masada.

How can I transmit the thrill of the young man from a *kibbutz* north of Acre who had the luck to find sections of the Biblical scroll of Leviticus?

The varying motives of the volunteers

Keenness of young Israeli volunteers

Or the reaction of the new immigrant, a young lad from Kibbutz Nahal Oz near the Gaza Strip, who was fortunate enough to discover a charred cooking-pot exactly as it was left on the stove when the woman tending it had been called away by the fateful resolve of the Zealots to end their lives? These were unforgettable moments.

Also interesting, though in a different way, was our experience with a group of new immigrants from North Africa, who had been sent to us by the Beersheba labour exchange for their first jobs. It was quite clear that they had not been briefed, not about the site, nor the expedition, nor the nature of the work, nor the difficult conditions. And I can still picture them as they arrived. They had been taken the wrong way and had done the stiff climb up the 'snake path' on the steep eastern escarpment of the rock, reaching the top puffing and panting, dressed in their Sabbath clothes and clutching their suitcases. Their desperate disappointment could well be imagined. They had been told they would be working 'in Masada'. But in Hebrew, 'Masada' spelt slightly differently but pronounced the same in their vernacular means 'restaurant', and here, instead of finding a bright and comfortable eating place – they were confronted by a stony hill in the heart of a desolate wilderness. Many did not stand up to it, and left. But those who remained learned to love Masada, and it soon meant to them what it meant to us. They turned out to be an excellent crew, and many even insisted on staying throughout the gruelling summer months, when excavations ceased because of the heat, to work on the restoration. Some of them continue at Masada to serve as guides and caretakers now that the site is open to the public.

Minimal discipline of camp Although we demanded no references from the volunteers – applicants were simply asked such particulars as their age, occupation, health condition and how long they wished to stay – among the thousands who came, we went wrong with only two or three, and these were sent home. All settled down beautifully and the discipline was exemplary. We did not of course run our compound as a military camp. We simply told them that if they got up in the morning on time and worked satisfactorily, they would be free to behave as they wished – except for the ban on leaving the camp without permission, because of the security dangers in the area. (We were only a few miles from the border.) For the rest, whether or not they kept their tents clean, whether they bathed or went dirty, it was up to them – and their companions. The system worked.

One of the problems of camp life was what to do with the volunteers during the long harsh evenings. The working day started at dawn and ended at three or four in the afternoon. True, we had warned them to come equipped with plenty of books; and members of our archaeological team and myself gave lectures on the history and archaeology of Masada and its surroundings – in addition to a thorough five-hour archaeological tour of the rock each Sabbath. We also brought in an occasional film, and guest artists from Tel-Aviv did a voluntary show once a week. But this was not enough. It was clear that entertainment to fill the vacant hours would have to come from the volunteers themselves, though it would not be easy to devise programmes to meet the tastes of people with different languages, cultural backgrounds, interests, and of different ages. Nevertheless in the second season they set up their own entertainments committee and their success was remarkable. A volunteer sitting next to me at one of the programmes said he doubted whether there was any other place in the world where so heterogeneous a group could sit together, sing together, and understand and enjoy the same entertainment as we were doing. Masada was without doubt the unifying thread. I particularly remember one such evening – it was *Hanukkah* (the Maccabean Feast of Lights) during our second season – when a *kibbutz* youth group put on a sketch at the foot of Masada. Boys and girls declaimed chapters of heroism from the chronicles of ancient Israel, and when they came to the episode of Masada, torches suddenly flared on the summit. We, standing in the shadows below, within the ruins of the Roman siege camps, gazed up, and it did not require much imagination to contrast the scene 1,900 years ago, when troops of the Roman Tenth Legion stood in their camps watching Masada burn, with the scene on this night, as we stood on our own soil, sons of an independent Israel, witnessing the torch of freedom set alight again atop Masada.

There is more that could be written about the volunteers. But I am concerned in this book with the archaeological discoveries of Masada. If, however, I have taken up space on the men and women who flocked to join us on the excavations, it is because without them and their enthusiasm we could never have uncovered so much, under conditions of such rigorous hardship. This book is therefore a token of thanks to my volunteer co-workers.

The excavations at Masada evoked echoes all over the world and particularly in Israel. It was perhaps fitting that the Government of Israel decided to commemorate this gigantic effort of thousands of volunteers – which had reached its peak after 125 years of research – by issuing a series of stamps and a commemorative medal. Each volunteer in the last phase of the excavations was given such a medal, bearing the short but expressive inscription: 'To the Volunteer'.

Bibliography

1 Flavius Josephus, *Jewish Antiquities, XIV; XV. The Jewish War, I; II; IV; VII.*

2 E. Robinson, *Biblical Researches in Palestine, II*, London, 1841.

3 S. W. Wolcott, *Bibliotheca Sacra, I* (Ed. E. Robinson), 1843, pp. 62–67; Cf. also: *The History of the Jewish War by Flavius Josephus*, A New Translation, by R. Traill, Manchester, 1851.

4 J. W. Lynch, *Narrative of the US Expedition to the Jordan and the Dead Sea*, Philadelphia, 1849.

5 S. W. M. Van de Velde, *Syria and Palestine*, Edinburgh and London, 1854.

6 F. de Saulcy, *Round the Dead Sea and in the Bible Lands*, London, 1854.

7 E. G. Rey, *Voyages dans le Haouran et aux bords de la Mer Morte*, Paris, 1860.

8 R. Tuch, *Masada, die herodianische Felsenfeste nach Fl. Josephus und neueren Beobachten*, Leipzig, 1863.

9 H. B. Tristram, *The Land of Israel*, London, 1865. *The Land of Moab*, London, 1873.

10 Capt. Warren, *Palestine Exploration Quarterly St.*, 1869, pp. 146 ff.

11 C. R. Conder, *Survey of Western Palestine: Memoirs, III*, London, 1883.

12 G. D. Sandel, Am Toten Meer, *Zeitschrift des deutschen Palästina-vereins*, 30, 1907.

13 R. E. Brünnow–A. v. Domaszewski, *Die Provincia Arabia, III*, Strassburg, 1909.

14 C. Hawkes, 'The Roman Siege of Masada', *Antiquity*, 3, 1929.

15 A. M. Schneider, 'Die byzantinische Kapelle auf Masada', *Oriens Christianus*, 6, 1931.

16 W. Borée, 'Masada nach der Eroberung durch die Römer', *Journal of the Palestine Oriental Society*, 13, 1933.

17 A. Schulten, 'Masada, Die Burg des Herodes und die römischen Lager', *Zeitschrift des deutschen Palästina-vereins*, 56, 1933.

18 M. Avi-Yonah, N. Avigad, Y. Aharoni, I. Dunayevsky, S. Guttman: 'Masada, Survey and Excavations', 1955–6, *Israel Exploration Journal*, 7, 1957.

19 I. A. Richmond, 'The Roman Siege Works of Masada, Israel', *Journal of Roman Studies*, 52, 1962.

20 Y. Yadin, 'The Excavations of Masada', 1963–4, Preliminary Report, *Israel Exploration Journal*, 15, 1965.

21 S. Guttman, *With Masada* (Hebrew), Israel, 1964.

22 Y. Yadin, *The Ben-Sira Scroll from Masada*, Jerusalem, 1965.

Index to illustrations